PERSPECTIVES ON VIOLENCE

Perspectives on Violence

Edited by

GENE USDIN, M.D.

Professor of Clinical Psychiatry
Louisiana State University School of Medicine
Director of Psychiatric Services, Touro Infirmary

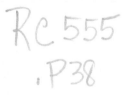

BRUNNER/MAZEL, *PUBLISHERS* • NEW YORK
BUTTERWORTHS • LONDON

Copyright © 1972 by The American College of Psychiatrists
Published by BRUNNER/MAZEL, INC.
64 University Place, New York, N. Y. 10003

Library of Congress Catalogue Card No. 75-179752

SBN 87630-047-6

MANUFACTURED IN THE UNITED STATES OF AMERICA

CONTRIBUTORS

HENRY W. BROSIN, M.D.
Professor of Psychiatry, University of Arizona College of Medicine; President, American College of Psychiatrists

WILTON S. DILLON, Ph.D.
Director of Seminars, Smithsonian Institution

H. STUART HUGHES, Ph.D., H.L.D.
Gurney Professor of History and Political Science, Harvard University

CHARLES PINDERHUGHES, M.D.
Professor of Psychiatry, Boston University School of Medicine; Director, Psychiatry Research, Veterans Administration Hospital, Boston, Mass.

HOWARD P. ROME, M.D.
Senior Psychiatrist, Mayo Clinic; Past President, American Psychiatric Association

NEVITT SANFORD, Ph.D.
Professor of Psychology, Wright Institute, University of California at Berkeley

LOUIS JOLYON WEST, M.D.
Professor and Chairman, Department of Psychiatry, University of California at Los Angeles; Medical Director, Neuropsychiatric Institute, UCLA Center for the Health Sciences

GENE USDIN, M.D.
Professor of Clinical Psychiatry, Louisiana State University School of Medicine

American College of Psychiatrists
1970-1971

Program Committee for 1971
Annual Meeting

vi

Contents

Preface

THIS VOLUME has evolved from the program "Alternatives to Violence" presented on May 1, 1971, in Washington, D.C., at the annual meeting of the American College of Psychiatrists. The primary papers are by a historian, a social psychologist, an anthropologist, and a psychiatrist, all eminent authorities in their field and all having the capacity to contribute to concepts broader than those pertaining to their particular discipline. An introduction by the then president of the College, Dr. Henry Brosin, who was serving as chairman, keynoted the speeches which followed. Two College members, Drs. L. Jolyon West and Howard Rome, rounded out and integrated the presentations of the four main speakers.

It is especially fortunate that participants in this symposium on violence are bridge builders to other interdisciplinary areas who not only can tell us much about human behavior we now experience in 1971, but can also give us insights into the structure, origins and processes of our current sociocultural and even political systems.

The speakers were afforded the opportunity of editing but were asked to preserve the spontaneity of their presentations. Because of time limitations at the meeting, they had to omit significant pertinent material from their talks; this material appears in the present volume.

Readers should bear in mind the specific date of the symposium. It was May 1, 1971, in Washington, D.C., a period during which our nation's capital was being disrupted by anti-war veterans and other demonstrators in a protest movement of which May Day was considered to be the climax. Charges of violence subsequently were hurled both at the demonstrators and at the "establishment."

Violence has become a fashionable topic for behavioral scientists—the literature on the subject is voluminous. These papers add a new dimension; certainly all the presenters speak out forthrightly and boldly. Much of their content will make the reader uncomfortable. An author's writings bear the stamp of his personal biography. This seems to be especially true in the area of violence.

The views of qualified social scientists, including many of our leading psychiatric colleagues, have been in direct conflict regarding the determinants of man's violence and destructiveness. For some, violence and destruction are viewed as being determined by inherent biologic factors, which, although adaptive to the "habitats" of man's earlier periods of development, have failed to change *pari passu* with his developing environment. The resulting anachronism has proved highly disruptive to contemporary society. Others have decried the classical concept of instinctual aggression, noting the lack of solid evidence in biologic observation. They would instead support an ontogenetic patterning of responses favoring collaboration rather than aggression. It can even be argued that violence is actually so alien to the human species that profound social and psychic programming is required for its legitimization.

In Professor Hughes' presentation, a note of "alternative to despair" may be seen. Here is another social scientist who has involved himself rather than simply remaining an observer. He has demonstrated by actions and participation just what his thought is. Hughes directly questions what many have held to be axiomatic, that successive acts of violence which have gone under the name of revolution had marked a major change in human events—and that this had been a change for the better.

Dr. Sanford makes us even more uncomfortable about a society which enslaves, murders, tortures or reduces the dignity of other people as a result of viewing the victims as less than human or beyond the pale of "civilized society." Urging a general theoretical approach, his paper is a brilliant and eloquent plea for utilizing developmental approaches in the prevention of destructive activities. His explorations, experiments and concepts have an immediacy which is most welcome.

Dr. Dillon invites a joint effort by anthropologists and psychiatrists to pool their knowledge of human behavior and to produce effective alternatives to international tensions and resulting hostilities. He brings us insight and guidance from other cultures which can be translated into concepts in our own area. Citing well over thirty authorities and recalling historical incidents, both ancient and modern, Dillon issues a "caveat" which is unmistakable: in both gift giving and in commercial exchange, never compromise the dignity of the recipient.

Dr. Pinderhughes brings us many heartbreaking facts which shake our complacency. With concrete observations and interpretations, he challenges psychiatry as to the worthwhileness of its concepts of aggression and related behavior. He notes that the aggressor must perceive his victim as a hated or evil object before he is able to attempt violence. He identifies some paranoid processes as non-pathological and considers these to be rooted in biologic patterns which cannot be eradicated. He offers 16 guidelines for better control of these processes. Some of his guidelines (e.g., learn to distrust what you see and hear and remember that reason more often leads one astray than to the truth) are bound to be more than provocative to many readers.

Some may argue that our society is currently testing the concept of the Hegelian superman: that if the ends are noble then the means can be justified and that this ultimately works for the benefit of all mankind. The atmosphere of violence prevails in our society although some maintain that it is diminishing. Many would decry a diminution in view of the injustices which they consider our society is not only condoning but also generating.

Violence can never be considered in isolation from history, past and present. Those of us who can take for granted the advantages of life we have in a political democracy must beware of smugness in decrying violence to achieve changes in a system which deprives the less fortunate of dignity, rights and benefits of the "democracy." When channels of access to political influence are blocked in a society, violence may be an effective means of expression and drawing attention. These papers present many ideas which are a challenge to our thinking at a perilous time for our society. The worthwhileness of behavioral scientists' concepts of aggression and related behavior can be attested to not only by their being deeply meaningful but also by these concepts being something more than exercises in futility.

This volume is the result of unstinting efforts by the Publications Committee of the College, including Drs. Charles K. Hofling of St. Louis, Henry P. Laughlin of Washington, D.C., Peter A. Martin of Detroit, John C. Nemiah of Boston, Melvin Sabshin of Chicago, and Harold M. Visotsky of Chicago. In addition, Dr. James P. Cattell of New York, a former member of the committee, has generously aided in its work. This particular committee has belied the adage that the chairman does all the work. They have been most diligent and cooperative in their responsibilities.

GENE USDIN, M.D., *Chairman*
ACP Publications Committee

PERSPECTIVES ON VIOLENCE

1.

Introduction

HENRY W. BROSIN, M.D.

THIS VOLUME, the third in a series, maintains the high quality of its predecessors. All of the essays are extremely useful in helping us better understand our patients in our daily clinical work and teaching because they furnish clear articulation of newly developing concepts and methods which are more appropriate to our current needs.

All of us are aware that our old formulations, however intelligent, need revitalization in terms of the new fashions of the current decade. No one would deny the value of longitudinal studies today even though it is more popular to stress the here-and-now aspects of the patient's complaint. We tend to forget that all of the leading teachers of psychiatry have also taught in one form or another the need to study the behavior of the patient in his current socioeconomic and psychological matrix. The dominant teaching of Adolf Meyer included the "I plus S equals R" formula to epitomize

3

the individual in a situation (social setting) reacting (reaction types). We have now new data and methods for studying human behavior. We have much more experience with clinical situations. Curiously, we are learning that the clinical pictures (syndromes) are changing and we must learn to deal with the new faces of deviance in more skillful ways. This is particularly true for the various cultures of poverty, youthful militancy, drug addiction and delinquency. It is in these areas of the larger world of affairs that our colleagues in the other behavioral sciences can be of great help to us even though we are responsible for the study of the breakdowns in human relations at the level of individuals, families, and small groups. Some of our colleagues, notably Erik Erikson in *Gandhi's Truth* (Norton, 1969), are becoming more skilled at understanding large group conflicts, but most of us do not pretend to excel in these areas.

The American College of Psychiatrists is developing the capacity to study the more complex questions in the fields of values and meaning, far beyond the usual daily clinical considerations. With perseverance we and our colleagues in other disciplines will make some small progress in the understanding of human behavior in all its puzzling complexity for the benefit of our patients, and perhaps for ourselves, even under the increasingly difficult conditions under which we live. To this end we will have to develop better concepts and methods for studying human behavior in more systematic fashions than we have to date.

For 2600 years the Greek ideals expressed in the Delphic sayings "know thyself" and "nothing in excess" have been known to us, but we have no single word for the concept "euphrosyne" discussed by Socrates in *The Charmides*, nor do we try to teach the methods for attaining controlled excellence over our passions, or living in a more comfortable symbiosis with the laws governing our inner life.

Freud expressed his pessimism about the ability of man to master his impulses under the conditions of large groups crowded together in his brilliant essay *Civilization and Its Discontents* (1927), which continues to have a current meaning even though it was written over four decades ago. Many physical and social scientists are persistently gloomy about the prospects of mankind, and it is not easy to refute them by hard data or logic. Uncontrolled population growth with its attendant malnutrition, increasingly destructive technology, deadly pollution in all spheres of living, and increasing rivalries among all nations lend credibility to those scientists who devise calendars for the dissolution of mankind.

Most of us are repelled by the view that we are helpless victims in the current struggle. As children of the Faustian Western tradition, we like to believe that we can do something active and meaningful about the human condition even though each individual man is indeed finite, mortal, usually frightened, and preoccupied with preserving existing security systems. We persist in our belief that our collective efforts may prevent the predicted apocalypse in spite of our celebrated internal and external conflicts, with their resultant symptoms and scars, our haunting fears of loneliness, poverty, pain, aging and death. Whether or not we are justified in our belief because our technology now is in an advanced state of excellence compared to former centuries will be a matter of history, but it is clear that we must study our problems and be willing to experiment boldly in order to set in motion those economic and socio-cultural forces which will enable us to survive. I like to think that these programs of the College, together with those of all other disciplines, are one small step forward on the immense journey toward a more just and livable civilization.

Our topic in this volume, "Perspectives on Violence," is

highly ambitious and controversial. There have been many
scientific and popular programs and books made available
during the past decade on various aspects of this multifac-
eted problem. Psychiatrists have had a long and abiding
interest in many forms of violence and its control on several
levels. Most of us recognize that the fact that we are born
as unacculturated biological organisms who require considerable training to become human is a central concept which
we cannot escape, much as we would like to. We all pay lip
service to the evolutionary story from Darwin to Julian
Huxley, but we are often apt to minimize the genuine hard-
ships in growing up, and the problems involved in "passion's
mastery." It is unpleasant to admit that we have a long
evolutionary history of cruelty and savagery, that most men
have been afraid much of their lives, were principally engaged in getting enough to eat, keeping away from predators,
and protecting themselves against the hostile elements. We
are genetically equipped for enormous adaptations, but we
evidently need to invent entirely new social mechanisms for
living together closely in large groups. As a race we have
survived much adversity, but it has been well asked, "Are
we able to survive prosperity?"

It is a question how much psychiatry as a profession
can contribute to the deep-rooted questions about methods
for changing human motivation and behavior. We can do
our best along with other behavioral scientists and human-
ists and mathematicians and physical scientists since no one
has assured answers.

It might be asked, "Why study alternatives to violence?"
While few would question its central importance and relevance to the current scene both at home and abroad, there
is a deep rooted pessimism among many of our citizens who
feel keenly the seeming impotence of the established church
and legal systems during the past decades, and the apparent

growth of uncontrolled aggression at both the individual and large group level. What can we say that was not known to our political and religious leaders throughout the centuries, or said by William James in his famous essay, *The Moral Equivalent to War?*

While in many ways the number and magnitude of the problems confronting us now dwarf all earlier conceptions of either external or internal control systems, it must be admitted that our means for dealing with these gigantic threats are enormously improved because we have a powerful technology which can provide, above all, information via many different media at all hours of the day or night, and thus shape public opinion in ways essential to the well-being of everyone on Spaceship Earth. Hundreds of writers have expanded on this thesis probably first expounded by Buckminster Fuller, but none has exceeded his grasp or his imaginative inquiries now codified as "The World Game." Many others have similar projects, and we can hope that from these efforts there will gradually develop concrete and tangible methods for dealing with problems of more limited scope. For example, Erik Erikson's *Gandhi's Truth* (Norton, 1969), on the origins of militant nonviolence, is a masterpiece which tells us in detail in a manner never before understood the ways in which such movements can occur and the psychodynamics of the individuals who make up such movements. We learn that the expenditure of energy of all concerned is very high and that highly disciplined action is required of many talented individuals, often at considerable sacrifice to themselves. Erikson's massive insights about the forces which move men and how they are guided by one charismatic leader, Gandhi, at a specific time under specified conditions can help all succeeding thinkers in their efforts to tackle projects which have dimensions that can be dealt with within the time and energies available, either now or in the near future. There are numerous study groups, including the well-known "think-tanks," working on these problems, and I believe that members of the College can add their insight, however modest, to the total effort. There are some highly informed and authoritative thinkers who, like Ramsey Clark, the former Attorney-General, believe that psychiatrists can add significantly to the current conceptions about delinquency, crime, drug addiction and related topics. While most of us would shy away from public statements as professional workers about nuclear warfare, overpopulation or the environmental crisis unless our professional work took us into those areas, it must be admitted that most of us are touched during our daily clinical work, at least at times, by many other threats to our well-being and the desired quality of life such as attacks on freedom of the press, strikes, police and official corruption, the breakdown of old conventions such as civility in the courtroom, youthful and black militancy.

Obviously, violence and aggression have many faces and there must be developed a multitude of attitudes and techniques to reduce the occasion for its appearance. With partial correction along the many fronts of poverty, inequities and social injustice, we will sooner or later find the definitions, the key loci for action, the appropriate experimental methods for determining somewhat better the alternatives to violence. We are beginning to understand that we can arrange the ways in which we live so that we need not destroy each other. Of course, massive alterations in our value systems will be required in order to change the economic system in such ways that there will become available immense new resources for human services. We need moral as well as material solutions to our problems because no one has good methods for changing social habits to save us from our own selfishness, egotism, intolerance, and prejudice.

Most of us know that we must learn how to manage the

irrational elements of our behavior in a rational manner. A realistic pragmatic, empiric approach seems to be our only reasonable course because we are not impressed by the simplistic solutions offered by communism, fascism, nationalism, or economic determinism. This attitude toward our worldly affairs is thoroughly in harmony with the relativistic, experimental exploratory, tentative methods developed in biology. We often cannot attain the certitudes which are found in the physical sciences, but we can use the trial and error method to find those approximations which serve us best, until better methods are found. We can retain our hope that the much celebrated mathematical model building techniques with computers which work so well for simple mechanical systems will gradually be perfected so that they will work more efficiently for large social systems. We know that the complex feedback from "multiple loop, non-linear mechanisms," which can be another name for intuitive social or political judgments, often do not work well because of unforeseen effects. This is all too clear in our environmental crisis, overpopulation, urban problems, and the fight against inflation-depression. The limitations imposed by human or political inertia upon systems analysis as applied to social systems is well demonstrated by the evidence marshalled by A. C. Enthoven and K. Wayne Smith, two of the most talented and energetic systems analysts working under Robert McNamara when he was Secretary of Defense. (*How Much Is Enough*, Harper and Row, 1971). They show that even though the fallacies of the "body count syndrome" and the attrition strategy, or the ineffectiveness of bombing North Viet Nam because Hanoi was able to make up its losses with less cost than Washington had expected were clearly evident from the data available, the governing bodies were unable to use this information. Obviously, more than technical skills are needed to provide the proper input into our superb calculating systems. We have the means but need the motivation.

Perhaps it would be well for a strong disclaimer to be entered here against the possibilities of predicting the outcome of any given course of action. Unfortunately, we are constantly being asked by many varieties of fanatics and "true believers" to accept one or another path to salvation. From long experience, and historians are most helpful here, we learn that monothematic or simplistic solutions are inadequate, bungling or even terrifying. We must learn to plan realistically, and not merely hope to escape into the future, however this may be conceived. I am impressed that so many young people (those under 25 years of age) are aware of the fallacies of the solutions being proposed by their militant colleagues. I wish more adults would be equally discerning. Most of us are now aware that even relatively modest innovations in technology may give us greatly improved tools for dealing with problems in genetics, pollution recycling and biodestruction, food and water production, new chemotherapies, energy transmission, and thus make possible entirely new strategies for dealing with seemingly difficult problems since the latter are too mammoth to respond to limited "miracles," but we can expect dividends from the concept of "the fertility of aggregates."

We need more basic science and a much better technology to rescue our civilization from its present impasse. There is no place to hide since the effects of our technology now reach the most remote deserts and arctic wastes. We need not despair, in spite of many who predict Doomsday for good reason, if we are willing to pay the price for the correction of the many threats to our survival. We have the concepts and the machinery to begin to correct these threats if we could motivate many of our fellow men to adopt somewhat different value systems. There is ample evidence from history that this has occurred in the past. While this does not mean it will occur now in time to save us from extinction, it does point out that the logical possibility exists, and that we might work at it.

In seeking even partial temporary "solutions" while we are developing methods for future explorations, I think we are in a strong position if we retain our psychobiological framework, but we must resist the strong temptation to seek simplistic, genetic or chemical solutions to behavior. Equally many of us are tempted to see "man" as a social construct who can be manipulated by current devices. Any student of modern ethology, anthropology or comparative psychology (see J. P. Scott "Biology and Human Aggression" *Amer. J. Orthopsychiat.* 40 (4) July 1970: pp. 568-576; "Emotional Basis of Social Behavior" also in *Annals of N.Y. Acad. Sci.*: Vol. 159: 777-790, July 30, 1969; and M. F. Ashley Montagu (Ed.) *"Man and Aggression,"* Oxford University Press, New York, 1968; See also Larry Ng (Ed.) *"Alternatives to Violence,"* N.Y. Time-Life Books, 1968; and J. D. Auerbach, and M. H. Miller (Eds.) *"Alternatives to Violence,"* Annotated references, Madison, Wisconsin, Dept. of Psychiatry, 1970; H. W. Brosin, "Human Aggression in Psychiatric Perspective" in C. D. Clemente and D. B. Lindsley (Eds.), *Aggression and Defense; Neural Mechanisms and Social Patterns, Brain Function,* Vol. 5, UCLA Forum in Medical Sciences, Number 7, University of California Press, Berkeley and Los Angeles, 1969, pp. 267-296) will recognize the fallacy of overly simplified models for behavior, and have growing respect for the much more sophisticated methods now being developed for the study of animal behavior. When we seek the causes of social behavior, it is now well established that there are many factors at several different levels from the molecular to the ecological. Any single-factor theory is inadequate, even at a single level of organization. Perhaps the gradual replacement of anatomical or structural concepts by process theory which is now occurring in developmental psychobiology will enable us to study "emotions" more intelligently. These newer methods and the insights they afford give us a much better view of the problems of controlling behavior than older models. But how to change social habits in existing human systems is the major challenge for which we are poorly prepared. Modern technology, within limits, can lead to "freedom from want."

There is now an unprecedented demand for the good life. Are all of us willing to pay the price required for this "ideal"? Federalization may carry severe constriction on personal liberty in order to make possible the social justice required. For example, can we invent ways to reduce overpopulation without severe infringement on personal liberties? Yet without such reduction we will probably have catastrophic famines in many countries. As suggested earlier in several different contexts, the difficulties in correcting the errors of our various economic, social and cultural systems are much more deeply rooted than we have known or have been willing to admit. Much of our culture is based upon wealth and privilege, and only slowly are we gaining recognition that many underprivileged groups, including women, blacks, youth and the poor, will not be able to share in the high enterprise of becoming more civilized, or more truly human without much help from those who are the privileged.

We have only superficial ideas about how to develop and maintain over time and through difficulties the essential humanness of a man. The traditional childrearing practices, educational, religious, humanistic, artistic, legal, governmental and "work" systems all have something to do with this delicate state of being. Various futurologists, including the more recent ones like A. Huxley (*Brave New World*), G. Orwell (*1984*), B. F. Skinner (*Walden Two*), warn us of the dehumanization which may occur with the triumph of technology and centralization. I would agree with René Dubos of Rockefeller University who has written well and extensively on these subjects (*So Human an Animal,* Scribners, 1968; *Man Adapting,* Yale Univ. Press, 1965, *Reason Awake,* Columbia Univ. Press, 1970; *The Dreams of Reason,* Columbia Univ. Press, 1961; *Mirage of Health,* Harper, 1959) that "mere survival is not enough for man." The creative potentials available to us are enormous, and tremendously important because we can design to some extent an environment which will favor the development of the best qualities we cherish in ourselves and in our fellow man. We can increase the degrees of freedom, however small at this time but greater in the next generation, for men and women to choose their destiny and the arena where they care to live their life with minimal lethal threat and maximum enhancement of their "humanness."

2.

A Historian's Critique of Violence from the French Revolution to Vietnam

H. STUART HUGHES, Ph.D., H.L.D.

WHEN I WAS a graduate student in history more than thirty years ago, we took revolutions very seriously. In particular we studied the French Revolution with respectful attention. We were convinced that on balance the revolution had been worthwhile; although we deplored its excesses, it never occurred to us to question whether something of the sort had in fact been necessary. We held it as axiomatic that the successive acts of violence which together went under the name of the revolution had marked a major change in human events—and that this change had been for the better.

A generation later, we are less sure. In the years immediately succeeding our graduate study, most of us served in a great foreign war, from which we expected that revolutionary alterations of society would emerge. Indeed, the years after 1944 did see a number of revolutions, but they were not of the classic variety—on the model of France in 1789 or Russia in 1917—that we had anticipated. There were Communist bureaucratic revolutions imposed from above in Eastern Europe; there was the military victory of Mao's armies in the Chinese civil war; there were wars of national liberation in Indo-China and Algeria; there was the nearly bloodless overthrow of a right-wing tyranny in Cuba. But in Western and Central Europe—the areas that most of us knew best—the suffering and social dislocation of the Second World War produced no major overturn. Capitalism and parliamentary government were propped up or restored, and bourgeois society, to the surprise of friend and foe alike, survived substantially intact.

More recently we have seen a military coup d'état in Greece, an evolution toward liberal practices brutally reversed in Czechoslovakia, and a series of student uprisings in Western Europe and the United States that have aped the gestures and the rhetoric of the classic revolutionary tradition. Most of us have condemned in one form or another all these events. We have ascribed to them little or no promise for a better future. More particularly we have been struck by the resemblances between the insurrections in our own universities and the sporadic, ultimately ineffectual movements that historians collectively call the Revolutions of 1848. We have found in them the same cult of spontaneity, the same fraternal euphoria, the same element of contagion, as the message spread from capital to capital (or university to university) that the discontented had risen in one center and that it was up to the like-minded elsewhere to follow their example, the same windy verbiage, the same confusion of words with acts, the same lack of clear or concerted goals, the same disillusionment as revolutionary alignments fell apart and the forces of law and order gained the upper hand. In 1968 and 1969 many of us felt for the first time that we truly understood what had happened a hundred and twenty years earlier. We now saw how it was possible for certain events to cause a great stir in history yet leave little trace behind. And concomitantly we were led to look more closely at movements we thought had in fact accomplished something—at the rare revolutions that had won the name of successes in contrast to the more numerous ones that had failed.

In the meantime other historians had been subjecting to critical scrutiny the revolutionary holy-of-holies itself, the epochal French events of the half decade 1789 to 1794. Recent scholarship has suggested that the changes effected by the "Great Revolution" were not so profound as had been conventionally supposed: in such crucial respects as the acceptance of democratic procedures and relations among social classes the decisive break-throughs seem to have come as much as three generations later, with the consolidation of the Third Republic in the late 1870's. If we accept this line of reasoning, if we look for signs of real democratization in the late nineteenth century rather than three-quarters of a century earlier, then we are bound to compare what went on in France with the situation in neighboring countries that had not enjoyed the blessing (if such it was) of a successful revolution. What we find there is the program of 1789 being carried out piecemeal at different rates in different spheres of endeavor, with France's neighbors gradually narrowing the gap separating them from the French precedent. By the mid-twentieth century, we may conclude, the gap closed entirely; today an imaginary observer knowing no history would find it impossible to detect from current practice which Western European nations derive their institutions from a revolutionary tradition and which do not.

If such be the historical record in Europe—and a corresponding conclusion might be drawn from the periodically deferred hopes for a better life in the Soviet Union—we are inclined to be equally skeptical about revolutions elsewhere. We suspect that the movements which now rivet our attention in the underdeveloped world may look considerably less important a generation or two hence; their leaders may likewise prove unable to cope with long-range social issues (such as an exploding birth rate) or to improve notably the conditions of the people in their charge. From the standpoint of history their exertions may appear over-valued; from the moral standpoint their accomplishments may seem incommensurate with the sufferings they have entailed. Here, as in Europe, a disabused observer may eventually decide that revolutions are significant not so much for what they actually do as for the legend that gathers around them. They live on in men's minds in the form of glorious memories, of an inspiration to heroic effort. As Georges Sorel realized more than a half century ago, what is important about a revolution, even a very great one, is not its achievements, which are always subject to debate, but the mythical "pictures of battles" it bequeathes to posterity.

The more dynamic among our students have come to the opposite conclusion. For them the Sorelian myths are the stuff of life itself. Precisely like the French historians of the Revolution of 1789, they take "the revolution" *en bloc* as something to be acclaimed or rejected entirely. They have no doubts of its morality; it is international war, rather, that they find immoral. One of the more curious of the generational cleavages which now divide the middle-aged from the young derives from opposing ethical judgments on violence. The students consider revolutions or civil wars justified—their professors seldom agree. We, on the contrary, find our rare examples of the moral application of violence in wars of national self-defense, in the Allied effort in the Second World War, or in the Six-Day Israeli campaign of 1967. But these two types of judgment are made with a

crucial difference. The young see the acts of violence they
approve as effecting some beneficent change, as having some
positive merit. We see ours in bleaker or more modest terms
as lacking any good in themselves, but directed toward preventing a still greater evil—and it is for this reason that we
find a resort to arms so seldom justified. Such distinctions
need to be borne in mind in assessing the alternatives to
violence that modern history suggests.

✓   ✓   ✓

Besides the ordinary processes of electoral and parliamentary action—and an endorsement of them is implicit in
all the foregoing—I can think of only two alternatives to
force of which we have any substantial historical experience.
The first is the disciplined, mass non-violence that Gandhi
called *Satyagraha*. The second is individual secession from
one's own community.

Satyagraha worked in India. It also worked to a limited
extent in the American South under the leadership of Martin
Luther King. But in both these cases the movements faced
established powers lacking determination or the sort of good
conscience that would have enabled them to apply counter-
force with utter ruthlessness. The British in India knew that
some kind of self-government was only a matter of time;
after blundering badly in the Amritsar massacre of 1919, they
shrank from actions that would produce further bloodshed.
The next quarter century was a period of step-by-step re-
linquishment of imperial authority, with Gandhi well aware
of the delicate game he was playing and quick to sense the
limits to the provocation that India's rulers would endure.

Similarly in our own country King and his followers enjoyed the advantage of confronting a divided official policy.
The segregation laws of the southern states contradicted
federal practice; those who violated local segregation or-

dinances could plead the defense that they were only trying to give reality to the supreme law of the land. Here as in India the entrenched authorities knew—although they were seldom fully conscious of it—that time was running against them; new people were moving into the South and a younger generation was growing up for whom the old segregationist slogans lacked their former evocative force. Yet despite these favorable circumstances, King's program is far from being accomplished. And he, like Gandhi before him, eventually succumbed to the violence that he had tried to exorcise from the national life.

Where established power has not hesitated, where the authorities have been resolved to suppress dissent at all costs, mass non-violence has not worked and has seldom been attempted. I know no examples of such protest against the fascist regimes in the interwar period. After the outbreak of the Second World War, there were isolated acts of courage like the Munich student revolt of 1943—but this was unknown to the bulk of the German population and was quickly snuffed out. In Italy the industrial workers of the northern cities resorted to mass strikes only after it was clear that the war was going badly for Mussolini and that the regime itself was tottering. The fall of the fascist systems came about not through the mobilized indignation of the peoples they ruled, but through defeat in a foreign war. And it has not been otherwise with the Communist regimes that have replaced the fascist as the leading exponents of authoritarian rule in our time. Only in Czechoslovakia in 1968 was organized non-violence tried against them, and this, after some initial success, was called off by the very leader, Alexander Dubcek, whom it was intended to support.

The more usual line of non-violent resistance to authoritarian government has been that of individual secession. Fascist Italy and Nazi Germany offer notable examples of men and women of principle who followed this second path. Most of them were intellectuals—and it is significant that in the Soviet Union today it is writers and scientists who provide the models for dissent. Yet individual secession—or "inner emigration," as the German called it—suffers under severe limitations. However courageous the individual who exemplifies it, he almost always knows where to draw the line. Few dissenters are willing to risk prison, fewer still death. Sooner or later on the path of protest, a prudent silence takes over. Still more, even at its best, such an act of secession means simply bearing witness to a truth contrary to the one officially promulgated. At its bare minimum, it may signify nothing more than a fastidious desire to keep one's own skirts clean. Whether boldly or cautiously practised, it can do almost nothing to affect the course of events. It is rather an effort to square one's relations with one's God or conscience—or perhaps to inform the historians of the future that there were a few chosen spirits in a time of evil who did not fall into line as they were told.

✓   ✓   ✓

These criteria for dissent may be useful in assessing our own current experience with protest against violence, the opposition to what we are now obliged to call the war in Southeast Asia. As an early leader of that opposition—and one whom events have now left far behind—I may be in an optimum position to speak of it with both the close knowledge of a participant and the detachment that comes from disappointed hope.

At the start it needs to be recalled that the protest against the Vietnam War was launched under favorable conditions. Although our country lacked the experience of opposition that the British had had with the Boer War and the Suez expedition, and the French with Algeria, there was an

American peace movement already in existence whose leaders knew each other and were accustomed to informal cooperation. To be sure their efforts had earlier focused on the thermonuclear danger, as in my own senatorial campaign of 1962, but the energies mobilized in such ventures could readily be transferred to the field of colonial conflict. Moreover, the temper of the population at large was less hostile to peace propaganda than it had been even a very short time before. On the international scene, the two years between the Cuban missile crisis and the Tonkin Bay incident had been the most relaxed of the entire post-1945 era. In the absence of alarms abroad, peace became a respectable issue. After the publication of Pope John's last great encyclical, *Pacem in Terris*, in the spring of 1963, American Catholic spokesmen began to modify their customary attitude of conservative nationalism. A few months later came the partial nuclear test ban and the hesitant coalescence of a "peace bloc" in the United States Senate. Stands which in the previous year had been marked down as politically suicidal could now be advanced with impunity; what earlier had been the wildest heresies were explained in terms of simple common sense on Capitol Hill. This was the era of such films as *Dr. Strangelove* and *Seven Days in May,* whose public showing—let alone their box office success—would have been unthinkable in the 1950's. The McCarthyism of those days now seemed no more than a bad dream; the advocates of peace were not afraid and had no reason to be afraid.

Hence when the bombing of North Vietnam in February 1965 gave the signal that President Johnson was embarking on a real war, the peace movement was quick to respond. The teach-ins of that spring alerted the academic community and a substantial part of the general public. By the following autumn, we were ready to launch the first of the demonstrations that brought tens of thousands of concerned citizens to Washington. In May 1966 we repeated the performance; as chairman of this second gathering, I drew attention to its good-humored, almost festive atmosphere and to the moderation of our stand. This line of argument, we thought, was the one that held most promise for the future: *we* were the responsible people, the true patriots; the President and his advisers were the extremists who were playing fast and loose with the interests of our country.

Our notion was a simple one and genuinely moderate—however bitterly we might condemn the war itself. We relied solely on the spoken and written word, on peaceful marches and advertisements in newspapers as evidence of our existence and our respectability. Our aim was to extend our following bit by bit from its original base among intellectuals until it would finally include the majority of our fellow-citizens. One day they would elect a Congress that would vote the country out of the war. Such a strategy demanded infinite patience; we knew that we had before us a very long march indeed. But we could see no alternative which would be non-violent in character.

How well did we succeed? The polls suggested that while the proportion of Doves in the population was mounting, the percentage of Hawks was increasing at a comparable rate and that the real change was a reduction in the number of the undecided. Moreover, under the heading of Doves there was carried a floating constituency which pinned its faith on negotiation. Negotiation, I recall, was the issue that bothered us most in these early years of opposition to the war; we were distressed to see how many of the advocates of peace subscribed to the slogan. To us total withdrawal from Vietnam, whatever its stages and modalities, alone made sense. Negotiation, we argued, had a fatal ambiguity—it could be espoused with equal fervor by both the Administration and its critics; the word lacked substance, when there was actually nothing to negotiate. Yet on balance we had succeeded beyond our expectations: we had made our opposition visible, and ordinary, cautious citizens ran almost no risks in joining us.

With such modest achievements behind us, we prepared for the presidential election of 1968. Naturally we were among the first to rally to Eugene McCarthy. And it was he who furnished us our only experience of triumph. Our supreme moment came with the New Hampshire primary and the stunned realization that we and people like us had knocked the President himself out of the race. The sequel is familiar to everyone—the candidacy of Robert Kennedy and his death, the Chicago convention, the election of Richard Nixon. The war went on—for what has already become three more years. After the McCarthy campaign, the democratic-minded, non-violent peace movement never recovered its momentum or its confidence. The war may some day end—but it will not be owing to the exertions of those who originally opposed it. It will come about through pressure from peace-minded Senators who, finally sure of their popular support, were ready to take over when the citizens' movement lost its bearings. A few years back I thought of writing an account of that effort entitled, "How We Won the War Against the War." Today I should have to write it in terms of a defeat.

In this kind of retrospect, it now looks as though the decisive change came a half-year before the New Hampshire primary, when the young and the impatient began to part company with the moderates. The march on the Pentagon in October 1967 was a confused and leaderless affair, but it inaugurated a new phase of direct action and vituperative rhetoric. Not only did the young people escalate the language of opposition and resort to physical assault on buildings or individuals that stood as symbols of the military establishment; they challenged the basic strategy of the peace movement. In place of the incremental tactics of slowly gathering electoral strength, they substituted the notion of sabotaging the war machine itself—even at the risk of civil conflict. I recall my utter incredulity when I finally understood what they were after, when I realized that they seriously proposed to bring the war to a halt by guerrilla action. The idea struck us as preposterous; when it came to fighting it out in the streets, the other side would obviously have more men, more money, and more guns. If our strategy demanded almost superhuman patience, that of the direct-actionists refused to reckon with the basic realities of American society.

Like its predecessor, this second strategy failed. The citadel of the war-makers declined to collapse. And by extending their campaign of incrimination beyond the war to other targets closer at hand, notably the universities, the young militants brought down upon themselves the wrath of the vast majority of their older fellow-citizens. Many of the latter drew away from further involvement with the cause of peace. Others—and this was my personal experience—were obliged to divert their time and energies to preserving their own academic institutions. The result was heartbreaking strife within the peace camp and a colossal waste of talent and good-will. It could only be a sign of the spreading unpopularity of the war itself that, despite the disarray among its critics, the number of its supporters continued to fall. It was a mark of the desperation of the American people that even some of the super-patriots began to argue for ending the war at all costs.

✓   ✓   ✓

From one standpoint, the opposition to the war in Southeast Asia can be seen as without precedent in modern history; never before had so many been mobilized in the cause of peace, nowhere else had the rejection of official violence been so articulate and so persistent. Yet viewed in terms of alternatives to that violence, the record of our recent history looks more doubtful. No technique emerged that achieved unqualified results; no consensus on procedure was reached among the war's opponents. The two strategies I have delineated were alike mixed in character and hard to sustain: that of the moderates lay somewhere between *Satyagraha* and individual bearing-witness; that of the young militants also derived from the tradition of mass non-violence while constantly threatening to spill over into terrorism. The perils of this latter course are too obvious to require elaboration. But we of the moderate persuasion should also recognize the force of our critics' charge that the way we chose was self-protective and platonic and that it seldom if ever entailed total commitment or willingness to die for one's beliefs.

There is a deeper reason for this lack of consensus—and one that suggests the almost insuperable difficulty of agreement on an alternative to violence in any context. What has been tearing the American people apart over the past half decade and more has been something that is not susceptible to cool scientific reasoning—nor to the kind of therapy that a discipline such as psychiatry can offer. It has been a clash of moral values, and these are by definition irreducible to scientific categories. One body of opinion among our fellow-citizens—and they may still be the majority—has held that the prestige of the nation comes before everything else and that the violence wielded in its name is ethically justified. While few intellectuals have understood this type of reasoning, our successive presidents have always had to reckon with it when they have faced the crunch of "humiliation." At the opposite pole, a smaller but highly vocal element has been convinced that violence on the part of the government calls for counter-violence—and that the resulting acts, whether on the part of North Vietnam, the National Liberation Front, or militants at home, are therefore moral in character. We alone of the moderate opposition have rejected violence without distinction: while condemning the atrocities committed by our nation's leaders, we have refused to condone those perpetrated by the "other side."

Thus we alone, I venture to conclude, have been fully consistent. Whatever our moral caution and our tactical failures, we have been even-handed in our judgments. We have argued that our country's war long ago lost whatever ethical justification it might once have claimed—and by the same token we have seen no virtue in revolution in the Third World. Our appeal has been to common humanity; our effort has been to limit the damage, to end the appalling hardship and loss of life among the peoples of Vietnam and Cambodia and Laos. No positive good, we suspect, can come from the withdrawal of America's armed power from those countries. But at least a frightful evil will have ceased; a goal will have been attained well worth the long, discouraging struggle against violence. The ethic that doubts one's own ability to do good yet insists on the overriding imperative of reducing human suffering—this ethic, I suggest, is one that the psychiatric profession as a whole shares with the moderate opposition to the war in Southeast Asia.

3.

Collective Destructiveness: Sources and Remedies

NEVITT SANFORD, Ph.D.

ATTACKS ON BLACK PEOPLE in this country—in the Algiers
Motel (1), at Orangeburg, South Carolina, at Jackson State
College, in Birmingham, at various Black Panther headquarters—the attacks on students at Kent State University,
and the massacre at My Lai (2) are, in their essentials,
events of the same order. There are differences among these
events in the size and power and representativeness of the
authorizing or legitimizing agency, and obviously in the scope
of the destruction, but all of them have this much in common: a group of people murders, enslaves, tortures or reduces
the dignity of other people (or another person), usually
in the belief that what is done is right, or at least necessary,
and that the victims are less than human or otherwise beyond
the pale.

Such events, of which human history offers us more than
enough examples, have been considered by my colleagues and

me as instances of sanctioned or legitimized evil (3). We
have used the word *evil* not to stand for an act or pattern
of life that is a sin or a crime according to some law but
to refer to social destructiveness of a degree so serious as to
call for the use of an ancient, heavily loaded term.

Most large-scale social destructiveness is done by people
who feel they have some kind of permission for what they
do—as we have called it, a sanction for evil. We have used
the word *sanction* in its more general, positive sense to
mean something that supports, authorizes, justifies, or legi-
timates an action, including encouragement given to an
opinion or practice by custom, public sentiment, or the like.

A common form of sanctioning occurs when nations or
powerful political groups persuade their citizens or members
that wars of conquest, imperialist or genocidal wars, the
indiscriminate killing or torture of opponents are right and
just, or at least necessary. States may do this through actions
by their legislatures, courts, or dictators. The most famous,
or infamous, case of this kind of sanctioning of evil was that
of the German Nazis, who displayed a great concern for
legality and managed to carry out their great atrocities by
first passing laws or obtaining court orders. Under such conditions, soldiers who shoot civilians or prisoners can say con-
vincingly that they were following orders and police officers
who torture suspects or fire into crowds can win official support for their claims that these actions were necessary.

We, of course, have no difficulty about calling the
Nazi atrocities evil even though they were in the narrow sense
legal; and we may well imagine that more than a few people
who accepted the atrocities or helped carry them out needed
and found more justification than mere legality. And so it
was, apparently, with the settlers who helped to put into
practice the widely held American view that the elimination
of Indians in the new territories of the West was necessary.

Consider an item from the San Francisco Bulletin of a little over a hundred years ago.

> Some citizens of this city, while hunting in Marin County yesterday, came upon a large group of miserable Digger Indians. They managed to dispatch 30 of the creatures before the others ran away (4).

We may assume that these hunters had no legal sanction for what they did: they had not been appointed to hunt down Indians. Yet we are not told that they suffered any difficulty in convincing themselves that what they did was legitimate and probably praiseworthy. It seems clear, then, that the legality or illegality of actions is not the only basis on which those who take part in them judge their acceptability. There are, in addition, processes of cultural sanctioning and of moral justification; and other "legitimizing" processes as well. Sanctioning refers to *all* the processes by which people, acting collectively, are led to feel, or lead themselves to feel, that evil actions are at least acceptable, appropriate, or necessary, even if not highly moral.

Sanctions for evil are not restricted to actions by states or large political organizations, but may refer to the behavior of a wide range of different kinds of groups, large and small. We need a general formulation that will hold not only for wartime atrocities and state-initiated programs such as genocide, but for lynchings, vigilante massacres, police riots, and certain forms of revolutionary violence. It may be particularly helpful to examine closely events such as those described by John Hersey in *The Algiers Motel Incident* (5). As many readers will recall, three policemen were arrested in Detroit for torturing and killing three young black men whom they were questioning about alleged sniping during a riot: in the young men's motel suite the police found no evidence of sniping, but they did find two white girls.

Along with physical assaults, legitimized evil can be said to include all collective actions that diminish human personality or prevent its development—actions such as enslavement, subjugation, oppression, exclusion, and discrimination against minority peoples. Ethnic prejudice or racism existing within individuals is a determining factor here, but the great evils are usually the work of groups.

Groups, of course, are of a great many kinds and sizes. There may be a group of two people; and from this, groups may differ in size and complexity over a very wide range— one that extends to the nation state itself.

It is instructive to consider a group of two. In Germany during the 1930s, after Hitler had seized power but before the extermination of Jews had proceeded very far, there was a revealing music-hall joke: a comedian says to his companion, "Show me a Nazi." Theoretically there could be one Nazi, and no doubt there was, but this story puts the proper emphasis on the social nature of the phenomenon, on the individual's need for external reinforcement of his Nazi outlook. Freud reported that when two SS men searched his apartment in Vienna he could easily make either of them lose face when the other was out of the room, but together they both made good Nazis.

If the presence of one other person can have so great an effect on the individual's behavior, we can readily imagine that the effects of, say, a dozen friends meeting face to face or of all the people in the organization where he works are sometimes profound indeed.

It has often been remarked that people are at their best and at their worst in groups. How do groups achieve their effects? What are the processes by which they influence individuals? What characteristics of groups—what functions, what forms of organization—have most to do with bringing about destructiveness?

Massacres, lynchings, tortures are usually the work of face-to-face groups, whose members are physically present at the same place at the same time. Here it is important to know how many of the participants knew each other before the event, and what were the relationships—such as leadership or fellowship—among them. In military and police organizations there are among the men who take part in illegal or evil actions formal relationships, depending on the roles the men occupy, as well as informal relationships such as friendships.

In our society, a prominent form of collectivity is the large organization—the corporation, the government bureau, the school or university. Here personality and social processes interact in the determination of destructiveness, for example, in what is known as organizational or institutional racism, of which the Nazi system of genocide and the American institution of slavery are familiar examples. Under these circumstances, apparently ordinary people, even people who profess opposition to the general trend of the system, contribute to an effect that is discriminatory or destructive merely by "doing their jobs." Hannah Arendt has dramatized this phenomenon in her book, *Eichmann in Jerusalem* (6). She used the term "banality of evil" to describe a state of affairs in which an apparently ordinary man, bent on doing his job efficiently and winning his promotion, could participate effectively in systematic mass murder.

Sociologists have long stressed the idea of the replaceability of individuals in bureaucratic roles, and used this conception to explain those common instances of corporate immorality in which blame can be attached to no individual. Organizational processes are clearly of enormous importance in maintaining racial discrimination in education, employment, housing, medical care, and the administration of justice in the United States. Small wonder that in much writing on this subject it is assumed that personality makes no difference. There is no doubt that organizations go their own way and that individuals adapt themselves to the requirements of their roles, but this is far from saying that personality factors do not enter into the determination of racist effects. Personality factors influence the selection of the individual for, and his own interest in, the role, his adaptation to it, the way he carries out his responsibilities, and the surrender of his individual conscience in favor of the organization's "morality." Individuals who cannot adapt themselves to the requirements of work in a school, hospital, social agency, or industrial organization leave, often after prolonged periods of unhappiness; and when organizations are caught in some blatant manipulation or discrimination or destructiveness, some individuals can usually be found who resisted the corporate action.

It is nevertheless understandable that people who are victims of organizational discrimination or destructiveness are not disposed to draw fine distinctions among the people who make up that organization. The white liberal who is shocked at being called a "racist" may in fact be taking his assigned role in an objectively "racist institution," quite unprepared for the cost of doing something to change it. Such tolerance of organizational racism is probably among the more subtle forms of prejudice not taken into account by existing ethnocentrism or anti-Semitism scales.

One way of approaching these phenomena would be to study ways in which individuals adapt to life in organizations. Are some individuals, under certain kinds of role requirements, more disposed than others to abandon their individuality and to become more cynical, to become, in other words, more dehumanized? And if so, does this kind of adaptation lead to a tendency to see *other* people as less than human? More concretely, we may expect that as young school teachers, welfare workers, and nurses lose their idealism and autonomy through convincing themselves that institutional actions contrary to principle are really all right; and as they thus become increasingly frustrated in their efforts to do anything for their charges or clients, they will take increasingly negative views of those they are supposed to help, and obtain higher scores on scales for measuring prejudice.

But organizations exist in society, and the values in accord with which they operate are widely shared in our culture.

The idea of widely shared values and needs seems necessary to explain why the policemen who were charged with committing the alleged murders in *The Algiers Motel Incident*, like the uniformed murderers of civil rights workers in Mississippi, assumed that nothing very serious would happen to them as their cases moved through the local courts; and to explain why they even felt aggrieved at being "singled out" in a way that led to their suspension from the force. As Friedenberg writes in his review of Hersey's book, "It is not, after all, customary to fine a dedicated officer for zeal beyond the call of duty; and, certainly, not for volunteering to participate, at some danger to himself, in a civic pageant designed to act out the fantasies of the populace" (7). In the prevailing culture of the United States aggressive impulses are strong though largely unrecognized, and a viable way of handling them is to participate vicariously in the aggression of officials against people who have been defined as morally low—usually, today, people of color, though students are another prominent target. This "fantasy," however, is not acted out except under special conditions, the most important of which are emotional excitement sufficient to impair the functioning of the higher mental processes and a barrage of propaganda depicting as less than human the people who are to become victims.

Defining people as less than human, or treating them as if they were perceived as less than human, has been termed by Bernard, Ottenberg, and Redl, "object-directed dehumanization" (8). From the annals of man's inhumanity to man there may be gleaned an enormous catalogue of dehumanizing appellations, from the worlds of inanimate objects, microorganisms, animals, witches, and devils. It has often been remarked that since in most cultures there are strong prohibitions against killing people—and in Christian societies against enslaving them—this process of defining them as outside the human race makes the killing or enslavement possible. Whereas any group of people who have become enemies, or been labelled as outsiders by a culture, may have dehumanizing imagery projected upon them, the objective characteristics of different groups of people may help to determine their selection as representatives of the persecutor's own "badness." Among these objective characteristics there might well be marks of earlier mistreatment at the hands of a dominant society. Minority peoples who have been the objects of genocidal attacks have usually been starved, deprived, cast out, generally reduced as human beings at the hands of occupying or surrounding forces or settlers; and then the effects of these actions were used as the basis for calling them less than human and so justifying their enslavement or elimination.

There is a close link between the dehumanization of others and "self-directed dehumanization" (9). If we regard others as less than human, or if our image of man is itself corrupt, we may harm them more easily than if we regard them as equals. Of course, dehumanization of a vituperative kind is not necessary for great destructiveness to occur;

nor do denigratory images of other people necessarily lead to physical acts against them. Destructiveness, however, is caused as much by social arrangements as by easily visible physical blows, and dehumanization takes many forms other than fearful abuse. For example, we may regard members of a particular group not as demons or germ-carriers or beasts of prey, but as machines or statistical units or child-men who need to be taken care of. We do not respect the autonomy of someone defined as incompetent, nor do we consider the feelings of people who are seen as machines with inputs and outputs and maintenance problems. This image of man may not trouble those who identify with the power of a "technetronic" future and who hope to stay on the right side of the control panel, but others will show how an impoverished view of man leads to straitened forms of life.

To some extent the present concept of dehumanization springs from the complex tradition surrounding alienation. When people are regarded as less than human by the dominant society, we are not surprised if they feel cut off from it; and they are joined as outsiders by those who see this dehumanization without being direct victims of it. It is important to realize, however, that dehumanization is not only a perception of others but a state of being suffered by those who feel compelled to treat others as less than human. Those who do this harm or who contribute to a system that does it may themselves be regarded as dehumanized, in the sense that they lack a sense of wholeness or a chance to develop aspects of themselves. In spite of this dehumanization, some of these people may identify strongly with the system, blaming their anxieties not on the hidden failures of their own society but on the threat posed by those who appear to be attacking it. In this sense, a dehumanized person may exemplify his society rather than being alienated from it. Similarly, he may avoid the discomforts of anomie, in the simple sense of lacking norms, by holding tightly to a set of norms which, for example, atributes all good to his own group and all bad to others. This, too, sustains dehumanization.

Although this process of "splitting" and projection accounts for much of the dehumanization around us, another kind may arise from corrupted images of man which the dominant group applies to itself and actually strives to fulfill. If, for example, a dominant group devotes itself overwhelmingly to techniques for achieving control and possession, it may so slight other aspects of life and other ways of relating to people as to deprive itself of values which it may not even know exist. If dissatisfactions felt by members of such a group are attributed to individual failure within its terms or to weakness caused by dissidents in the system or simply to a momentary lack of goods which that system might eventually provide, members may resist any change or expansion of their image of man, in spite of their own infelicity. In a system such as this, members are dehumanized by their own way of life, even if nobody on the outside regards them as deprived of significant human possibilities.

If dehumanization can refer both to a view taken and a life lived, what is the relation between these two senses of the word? Each of these senses can refer either to the self (or to one's own groups) and to others. Thus, we may learn or fashion denigratory images of ourselves as well as of other people. In some cases others may teach us a bad self-image, which serves as a means of social control: "black is beautiful" often seems to mean "we are good or could be if you would get off our backs." Dehumanization as a view taken, either of the self or of another, could be revealed and measured in a number of ways. Scales developed for the study of prejudice, authoritarianism, or self-esteem, together with clinical studies, measures of ego growth and of moral development, and instruments for eliciting basic images of man, all suggest methods for a more sensitive study of dehumanization as a perception or attitude.

Dehumanization as a condition of life, apart from perceptions by the participants, calls for additional kinds of measures. Investigation of it is necessary, even though work in this field obviously deals with values. It is necessary if we are to examine the links between images and actuality, and if we are to avoid suggesting that the problem is solely psychological. For example, one person may wrongly blame all his troubles on a society which is said to dehumanize him, or another who actually is dehumanized by his conditions may fail to realize it. Even if the perceptions of both are corrected, say by psychiatric means, they will still have their troubles. Moreover, perceptions of one group can help to perpetuate the dehumanized way of life suffered by another group. For example, if a significant group of white people regard most blacks as shiftless, dangerous, stupid, or immoral, and if these perceptions have any influence on public policy or private behavior, the blacks will suffer and lose opportunities to develop as full human beings. To the extent that some of the victims are actually corrupted by these policies or by a less than benign neglect, the dominant group may find evidence for its perceptions. Meanwhile, whites who engage in this sort of defensive and condemnatory thought are themselves dehumanized by their absorption into a world peopled by stereotypes. To what extent do racists suffer dehumanization of one kind in the process of engaging in another?

To answer this kind of question, we need a model of human development. Our model can remain loose, inclusive, and open, but in order to see the deprivations that people suffer we need a working image of what man can at best become, of salutary kinds of development. We would not wish to restrict this model to a narrow or time-bound version of humanism. We would include ideas of self-actualization and of psychic integration, of diversity and wholeness. In using the word dehumanization, we refer to either a denial of this potential or a deprivation that impairs its realization or even induces regression. Correspondingly we view "humanization" as the process through which a person approaches, at each stage, the best of which he is capable. With an open model of human development in mind, we want to ask, for example, in what ways does a failure of development lead to behavior that impairs the development of others, or to denigratory attitudes toward them? In particular, what kinds of experiences lead to reliance on a psychological disposition to destructiveness?

This disposition differs both from the impulse of aggression and, in its scope, from the act of violence. As a disposition it binds together a motive, a kind of object, and a mode of action. Acts of violence narrowly defined are easily recognized, classified under a single heading, and even counted, but the motivational sources of violence are extremely diverse. There is a long-standing psychological proposition, supported by numerous experiments, that aggression, including its violent manifestations, is provoked by frustration; and everyone can think of many sources of frustration he encounters. In the case of destructiveness, in contrast, it is the acts that are diverse while the motivational source is a single complex disposition. As suggested above, destructiveness can occur by symbols or by social arrangements as well as by violence. (Although some writers with whom I essentially agree have stretched the word violence to cover non-physical acts of "violation," such as violations of dignity, I hope to avoid confusion by using the word violence in its ordinary, narrower sense.) Thus, destructiveness can appear in forms as diverse as polite social discrimination or a massacre of the innocents. Its basic aim is to get rid of some person, whether by excluding him, ignoring him, or reducing him to less than human status, which in the extreme means death. That is the motive. The object of this disposition is people (or aspects of them, or objects that represent something human), and in particular those who are perceived as bad, low, alien, dirty, immoral, or otherwise threatening. Its modes of action include psychological mechanisms and social practices which make people disappear or lose their status as people. Victims are made to feel, as black literature makes clear, as if they were invisible or nobody knew their names. They hardly exist.

Unlike "instincts" such as the aggression described recently by some popular writers, destructiveness is not inborn but is generated out of experience and learning in a social environment (especially out of the punishments, terrors and "final solutions" of childhood). Fundamentally, its source is inner conflict, leading to a need to get rid of what is all-too-human in one's self. If this badness is felt to be located in the self, a person may become self-destructive; but often he may ascribe this badness to other people, upon whom the conflict is then played out. Although this process may induce a moralistic sense of rightness, it seldom removes the lurking sense of one's own badness; and even if it did, the social cost is staggeringly high. As an adaptation to human problems that many of us face, destructiveness is a dangerous failure; but in seeking alternatives we may derive hope from its status as a learned adaptation, not an instinct.

But, as has been shown, it will not do to rely solely on psychological explanations of collective destructiveness, the act of doing harm together. It is clear, for example, that ordinary decent Americans will do great harm if given certain sanctions. Here we have in mind not bombings of Vietnam, but a series of experiments run by Milgram on what he called obedience. Large majorities of university students and of townspeople pushed switches which they thought gave severe and dangerous shocks to people who failed to supply correct answers in what was described as a learning experiment. Even when the victim groaned in pain, announced that he had a heart condition, and demanded to be let out of the experiment, most of those seated at the control panel continued to follow the logic of the experiment and the comment of the psychologist that "you have no choice." In this case, of course, they could simply have got up and walked out, as some people did, but most of them obeyed. We must assume either that an extraordinary percentage of the sample was highly disposed to destructiveness, or that severe social destructiveness may be carried out by people who respond less to hatred toward the victims than to the guidance or commands of superiors. To the extent that the latter is true, it is important to investigate dispositions to submit to what others ask, or at least to acquiesce in what they are doing. And again, we must look not only at the dispositions but at the social structures which help to create them and which make use of them. In each case, we must also study the exceptions, such as a disposition to question an authority whose commands violate important values, to seek changes in the system, and to resist if necessary.

I may summarize what has been said about collective destructiveness by returning to the question of how massacres happen. A general formulation is as follows. Individual conscience is replaced by a collectivity, or powerful individual, having the power to say what is right, what wrong, what good, what bad, who is the enemy. This makes possible a release of primitive aggressive impulses with their related imagery. Both of these changes in individuals are made possible by failings—in the higher mental processes or ego functions, which in turn are due to the fear, fatigue, and confusion of the moment and the behavior of other members of the group that carries out the destructive action.

At the same time massacres such as My Lai have to be understood in the light of the general military policy that, however implicitly stated, lies behind them; and in the light of cultural trends that make such policy seem legitimate.

Our concern, however, is not primarily with massacres and legitimized murders but with the general destructiveness of which such events are particularly horrid manifestations. This destructiveness takes many forms, ranging from social discrimination to mass bombing of civilians.

For the sources of this destructiveness we have to look to the American ethos and to the ways in which its darker features have been brought to the fore by the present crisis in our society. And we have to look to the depths of the human psyche.

The darkest trend in our ethos is that which extols our goodness and purity while ascribing all manner of evil to foreign and domestic minorities, who are thus marked for exclusion, suppression, or elimination. This trend parallels and is related dynamically to the psychological tendency to deny, to cut off from oneself, various natural impulses that are felt to be bad. Resistance to collective destructiveness must, therefore, take the forms of promoting universalism in the human community and wholeness in the individual personality. Universalism means most essentially accepting and appreciating cultural diversity while recognizing common humanity; wholeness in personality depends most heavily on accepting, making a part of the self, and turning to non-destructive purposes, basic emotional impulses. Progress toward one of these objectives will favor progress toward the other, for universalism and wholeness are mutually dependent: acceptance of one's self favors acceptance of other people while the emergence of hitherto suppressed minorities and peoples, the rise of "counterculture," and the strengthening of intellectual and moral resistance to racism and imperialism can help to revive and to reconstruct the humane and humanistic trends in the American ethos, and when these are fully expressed in official policy—particularly in education—individuals will be better able to accept themselves. It is within this broad framework that we should view the question of how acts of collective destructiveness can be prevented.

Prevent, however, is not an adequate word for what we want to do or for what is needed. It is not enough to prevent dehumanization and destructiveness; a more worthy goal, and one just as obtainable, is to *humanize* and to develop *constructive* relationships among people. This is not merely toying with words, or reversing emphasis in order to attain to an optimistic view. It can be shown that it is in the nature of planned action affecting people, whether singly or collectively, that if it is to do more good than harm it must be guided by positive values. This follows from the fact that in both individuals and social systems we deal with organized complexities, with numerous interacting elements or features. A change in one of these elements or features, be it a virtue or a fault, a strength or a weakness, will bring desirable or undesirable changes in other areas of the person or system and actions directed to one feature of the totality are likely to affect others in various ways, some good and some not so good. For example, a mother's attempts to prevent her young son's displays of aggressiveness could impair his sense of masculine identity; a school's efforts to promote competence in a particular child can reduce his creativity and spontaneity and block his social development; a university's efforts to prevent militant activism by some of its students may easily promote activism in most of its students, or else suppress the spirit of inquiry throughout the institution; what a nation does to prevent its people from thinking the wrong thoughts is likely to impair all their thinking.

This means that actions must be based in an understanding of the whole, and actions concerned with specific features of the person or social system must be consistent with a conception of the well-being of the whole. The best overall strategy is to direct improving and promoting activities to features that have determining relationships with most other features.

In an important sense, the whole with which we are concerned embraces both personality and culture. The relations between the two are so intimate that it is impossible to tell which comes first. Just as the idea of the individual's incorporating social norms is necessary to an explanation of personality development, so is the formulation of ways in which individuals manage their impulses and inner conflicts necessary to an understanding of how culture is generated. Activities to change personality and activities to change culture are, essentially, of the same nature.

Changing personality and culture are, to be sure, relatively long-term processes, but we do not have to wait until the next generation has been raised before more humane and constructive personality dispositions can come to exist in our people; personality-developing activities, affecting adults as well as young people in large numbers, can be undertaken now. And well-directed actions to improve the institutions primarily responsible for shaping personality in children, i.e., the family and the school, will also improve these institutions.

One place to begin an effort at social and cultural change, to build a microcosm, as it were, of a larger effective program, is with helping parents to do a better job with their children. Such an effort need not be limited in its aim to producing a better future generation; it would, properly carried out, have beneficial effects upon the personalities of the parents themselves and, at the same time, be likely to improve those who carried it out.

Let us consider an example. Community colleges that are fully to serve people of the inner city must have facilities on the campus for taking care of the children of mothers who need and want to attend those colleges. Some of these mothers and other students would work in these centers, and this work would be integrated with formal and informal instruction in child development and child care. It would be assumed by instructors, and it would soon be taken for granted by all concerned, that mothers or other students who wanted to understand and do what was needed for the children would first have to understand themselves and change some of their value-orientations. This understanding and change would be furthered by the fact that it had community support. And the mere presence of children on campus would help to make the whole college more of a human community. All hands would be reminded of what they were and what they might become. The mere fact of being in college would be a boost to the self-esteem of the mothers and an important step toward their liberation from men; and this would be for the latter a crucial step toward *their* liberation from male chauvinism and authoritarianism.

Some say that for this to happen our culture would need to have changed already, but we have to start somewhere, and it seems more reasonable and more hopeful to set about instituting a child care center at a community college than to set about changing our culture. If, however, what was done at this college became a model for a hundred other colleges, there probably would be some impact on culture; and even if it did not become a model, it would still be worth doing because of its intrinsic values.

Programs such as this should aim at personality development in general and be guided by a theory of development. We need, as Bellah argues, "a conception of man which will allow us to accept our darker side, to use creatively our id impulses, our dependency needs and our rebelliousness rather than projecting them on others and then murderously repressing them" (10). Broadly inclusive humanism not only counters directly the evil we have been discussing but it is a vision of fulfilled human potentiality.

Other, not dissimilar, visions have been offered in recent years by such psychologists as Erikson, White, Maslow, Barron, Jahoda and Allport (11). My own thinking about human potentiality and how it might be developed is based mainly on a study of education beyond the high school, but it agrees with what others have written about earlier development and also about growth outside of formal institutions of learning. I would say that a high level of development in personality is characterized most essentially by complexity and by wholeness. In general terms this means that a large number of different parts or features have different and specialized functions; and also that communication among these parts is great enough so that, without losing their essential identity, various parts become organized into wholes in order to serve the larger purposes of the person. The highly developed person enjoys a rich and varied impulse life. His feelings and emotions are differentiated and civilized; his conscience is enlightened and individualized. It operates in accord with the individual's best thought and judgment. The processes by which he judges events and manages actions are strong and flexible, being adaptively responsive to the multitudinous aspects of the environment, and at the same time in close enough touch with the deeper sources of emotion and will so that there is freedom of imagination. This highly developed structure underlies the individual's sense of direction, his freedom of thought and action, and his capacity to carry out commitments to others and to himself. But the structure is not fixed once and for all. The highly developed individual is always open to new experience and capable of further learning; his stability is fundamental in the sense that he can go on developing while remaining essentially himself.

Particular value orientations of this kind are easy to criticize, for they are frequently bound by culture, social class, or historical era. But the answer to this criticism is not ethical neutrality, but a fresh attempt to think well about values. The search for worthy values must go on, and if social scientists are to assist in designing plans for the up-bringing and education of children, they must be guided by open-ended conceptions of what people can become. Even while committing themselves tentatively to particular systems of value, they can continue their efforts to improve thinking about values by showing how values are arrived at and what will be the consequences of particular values.

A reasonable course for the scientist or educator who wishes to avoid dogmatism is to start with some attribute of the person that no one will deny is *a* value, and to set about promoting it without immediately raising questions about its place in a hierarchy of values. He would be on safe ground today if he began with *competence,* for example. If he accepted the view that virtues, like illnesses and weakness, are not isolated in the person, he would soon discover that actions to promote competence had consequence for other qualities. Competence is often attained at the expense of other desirable qualities; but is this sacrifice really necessary? Intellectual and emotional development can, indeed, be regarded as aspects of the same process; and it ought not to be beyond our competence as educators to make arrangements whereby various aspects of the person develop in concert.

How people develop is less a subject for controversy than what they might become. Among psychologists there is not much disagreement with the general principles that people develop when they are both confronted with challenges that require new adaptive responses and freed from the necessity of maintaining unconscious defensive devices. Of course, the challenges must be within the limits of the individual's adaptive capacities; if strain is too great it will induce a falling back upon primitive, anti-developmental responses. And concerning making the unconscious conscious or increasing self-awareness it must be pointed out that, except in cases of severe disturbance in childhood, special psychotherapeutic action is rarely called for; educational procedures can help make people aware of their impulses and defenses, and these procedures are the more effective the more the personality as a whole has been expanded through appropriate challenges. These general principles hold for adults as well as for children and adolescents. People can develop at any age if the right conditions are introduced.

The authors of *The Authoritarian Personality* (12) were not backward about making proposals for child training that could help to prevent the development of authoritarian personality trends. "All that is really essential," they wrote, "is that children be genuinely loved and treated as individual humans." They assumed that lack of love is a fundamental cause of aggression, and that authoritarian discipline was a formidable barrier in the way of ego development. They argued that discipline that is strict and rigid and, from the child's point of view, unjust or unreasonable may be submitted to, but it will not be fully adopted in the sense that the child will eventually apply it himself in the absence of external authority. Where the child is not allowed to question anything, to participate in decisions affecting him, nor to feel that his own will counts for something, the stunting of the ego is an inevitable consequence.

It seems fair to say that these perspectives on upbringing have long been shared by most professional people who, in various formal and informal ways, are involved in the education of parents. One may go further and say that there is a vast American literature on child development, much of it addressed directly to parents, that goes far beyond cautions about authoritarianism in setting forth general conditions for healthy development. It is possible to summarize much of this literature by saying that children need to be brought up in an atmosphere of trust, love, justice, freedom, and truth.

Trust in someone is absolutely necessary if the child is to learn the most elementary facts about the social world and to establish those stable relationships upon which basic inner stability depends. The child must be loved if he is to develop the self-esteem and sense of identity that will enable him to love others in a genuine way. Justice is the cornerstone of faith in the human community; its denial to a child is a major stimulus for aggression and unbridled self-seeking. Unless a child or young person feels that he is justly treated, he will not care about freedom; and he must have freedom, in amounts suited to his stage of development, if he is to have experience in making choices, and this experience is requisite to his becoming an autonomous person. Truth is the overriding value. The child must learn to appreciate it and live according to it if he is to gain any understanding of, and therefore some control over, himself, and work with others in gaining control over his environment. He can be taught only by example.

These considerations afford a perspective in which to view aggression in children. The element of aggression in collective destructiveness is extremely remote from any "instinctual aggression" or the aggressive propensity that a child brings into the world; any aggression manifested by an adult is always a result of much shaping through experience and always interacts with other learned tendencies such as obedience, conformity, striving for masculine identity, and defining victims as less than human.

This is not to say, however, that the anger of the frustrated young child is not largely an expression of an inborn potentiality. But this in itself is not something for the parent to worry about. As parents, we do not want children to be incapable of anger or never to express any; we want them to learn to be angry about the right things (human exploitation, for example) and to express their anger in ways that will help counter destructiveness. The passionately non-violent mother fails her child when she responds with horror to any display of anger by him and sets herself the task of totally suppressing his aggression. She forces the child to direct his aggression against himself and thus to bear guilt that properly belongs to her.

The child's natural potentiality for aggression does not become a source of destructiveness toward himself or others until aggressive impulses having specific objects and modes have been built up through experience. The crucially important experiences are of losses or denials of love, of weakness and humiliation, of unjust punishment, of threats of bodily harm—experiences which the child interprets as having catastrophic implications. Love and gentleness and firmness are the counters to such experiences, but such are the exigencies of childhood that the generation of some aggressive impulses is virtually unavoidable. The child will still need the parents' help in learning to control these impulses, to express them in relatively non-destructive ways.

However we might conceive of the contributions of nature and of experience to the generation of the child's aggression, it is wrong to assume that there is some "store" of aggression which has to be drained off in one way or another. Even in children noted for their "meanness," who seem ready to be aggressive on slight provocation, this does not seem to be the right formulation. Aggression, far from being drained off, is likely to become its own stimulus, for aggressive behavior leads to feelings of guilt which may be suppressed by more aggression. Aggressive behavior has a great diversity of meanings. There are various (often quite specific) internal readinesses-to-be-aggressive that are triggered by external events which are not so much obviously frustrating in themselves as evocative of long-standing susceptibilities to humiliation, feelings of powerlessness, of being catastrophically threatened, and so on. An observer can hardly hope to find the meaning in every case—nor can the subject himself. The best strategy for coping with this state of affairs, on a long term basis, is a program aimed at building self-confidence, competence, adequate masculinity, and self-awareness.

A major stimulus for the generation of aggressive impulses in children is unjust punishment at the hands of repressive authority. Yet, children brought up by stern or carelessly punitive parents rarely become courageous rebels; instead, they are likely to become authoritarian. For the young child such parents are seen as dangerous, and he learns quickly enough to suppress his aggression against them, even to tell himself that they are not bad but good, and to redirect his aggression against people who do what he himself would like to do but cannot. Does this mean, then, that parents should never punish or forcibly restrain their children? If not, how are they to distinguish between the use of force that is wise, or just, or at least necessary and that which leads to authoritarianism? Must they be either sternly punitive or "permissive?"

Here it is necessary to distinguish among styles of authority and to consider parental control in relation to the child's stage of development. Parents by law and custom are in a position of authority, i.e., they are vested with the right to command obedience, respect, and confidence. How they go about carrying out the responsibilities of this position varies widely from one family to another. Many parents, unfortunately, are not well qualified for the position they have seized or had thrust upon them; out of indifference, or neglect, or ignorance, some offer the child too little authority or régime; this is experienced by the child as a lack of love and as untrustworthiness in the world at large, and hence it is a major source not of authoritarianism but of the most serious kinds of psychological disturbance. Other parents practice an authoritarian style of discipline; unsure of themselves, afraid of their own impulses, over-eager to have their children conform to conventional standards, they make many rules, try desperately to stick to them, over-react to the child's failures to conform. In general, they conduct themselves as parents more in accord with their own unrecognized psychological needs than in accord with the needs of the child. This is very different from the flexible use of authority to supply guidance and support as needed.

Young children need authority, but as they grow older this need diminishes gradually. Parents, it seems, have great difficulty in adapting themselves to the changing needs of the child. Strong believers in authority tend to favor authority in all times and places, regardless of the needs or circumstances of the developing individual, while strong believers in freedom, in respect for the child's individuality, tend also to develop a total ideology and to underestimate the young child's need for authority. It will help parents to find the right approach if we ask, once again, what, in a positive sense, we desire for our children and how do children in fact develop.

In a democratic society we value independence of judgment. We want people to grow up to become their own authorities. We recognize, however, that this is a difficult accomplishment, for everybody at some time experiences a need for some kind of authority. Young children need it most and can tolerate it best, adolescents need a lot of authority but have very little tolerance for it, while the ideally developed person needs relatively little and can tolerate it well.

Whatever parents might do—to generate authoritarian personality trends or to set the child on the road to full development—can be profoundly altered, favorably or unfavorably, by the schools. This seems generally understood, for in America practically everybody is willing, even eager, to offer his opinion about what the schools should do and how they should go about it. About the only thing that seems generally agreed is that school should produce good democratic citizens—informed, useful, concerned, and loyal Americans. How this is to be done is a subject of much controversy, and official statements of policy are often contradicted in practice.

Such controversy seems inevitable, for educational institutions, which involve nearly a third of our people as students, teachers, and administrators, are fully expressive of our culture, with all of its conflicts and contradictions. What the public schools actually do seems, on the whole, quite in line with what most people of the great middle class think they want them to do. Education is thought of as a scarce commodity and access to it is according to a system of merit, usually degree of conformity with middle class values and ways; the process of education is defined as the acquisition of skills and knowledge, which is to be accomplished in the most efficient way possible; achievement is the highest value, and this is measured in terms of performance within the system of prearranged goals and tasks.

Yet almost nobody is happy about the schools. Most unhappy, no doubt, are the students, who in 1969 brought about serious "disruptions" in two-thirds of city and suburban and half of the rural schools in the country. These disruptions upset a large segment of the tax-paying public, who demand more of the repression which made the students unhappy in the first place. Caught in the middle and severely frustrated are most teachers and administrators, and all parents who have some understanding of what education for democracy really means.

The trouble is surely connected with the fact that the public schools are guided mainly by the belief that their task is efficiently to impart knowledge and skills; children are to learn how to be democratic citizens, presumably, by learning the facts about democracy. This belief and the procedures based on it have had some success in the past, not because the skills and knowledge imparted had much to do with democratic behavior—though they were useful enough in other ways—but because schools were more or less democratic institutions and were manned by men and women of humanity and goodwill, as they to a large extent still are. In times of rapid social change and great controversy, however, "teaching the facts" becomes the only defense against involvement in controversy, yet it is precisely such involvement—"relevance"—that students and many parents demand. Today, schools are confronted not only with conflicting ideological pressures from without and within, but with enormously expanded enrollments and greatly increased diversity of students in the same school and the same class. The reaction has been greater organizational rigidity—more and more rules, which are more and more rigidly enforced.

Presumably what goes on in the schools is still called education for democracy. Yet it seems fair to say that the basic requirements of such education (trust, love, justice, freedom, and truth) are largely sacrificed to a desperate need for immediate order. Students are still acquiring some prescribed knowledge and skills, but we may be sure that much of their learning is, as always, by the example of their elders. This being so, it is not surprising to find, as we do, that students who do not rebel arrive at college with marked dispositions to authoritarianism.

For turning our culture in the direction of humane and democratic values nothing is more important than reform of our schools. Nobody knows how this is to be done, but it is possible to offer some suggestions.

In the first place, it must be recognized that although schools probably need some kind of structure, they certainly do not have to be authoritanian. The authoritarian style is not in the nature of human organization but is to be understood as a patterned reaction to circumstances. An organization as a whole will tighten up in response to external threats, and as it does individual teachers and administrators will exhibit more and more authoritarian behavior, thus affecting directly the young people in their charge. The classroom teacher need not be more authoritarian by disposition, or more incompetent, than the average in order to be provoked into totalitarian behavior by a class that seems about to get out of hand or by a principal who is insistent upon order at any cost. That principal may behave as he does because of his fear of the superintendent, who, in turn, is afraid of the school board. But if a school system as a whole is moved in an authoritarian direction in this way, it can also be turned in a democratic direction by strong leadership from the top —by the superintendent or the board.

At the same time, individuals, though heavily influenced

by the system, are not totally determined by it. A principal with courage and resourcefulness can still do much to determine the climate of his school, and a teacher of high competence and determination can still have a class that is democratic in spiirt. Indeed, it is largely to the presence of such people in the schools that we owe the fact that these institutions, in spite of everything, are turning out some of the best young people that this country has known.

It is also in such people as these that we find expression of truly impressive counterforces to authoritarianism. If the present is a time of great tension and rigidity in the schools, it is also a time of much soul-searching and innovation. It is not only students but teachers, researchers, and administrators who complain of the impersonality, lack of relevance, and stultifying bureaucratic processes of the schools. For reform to occur it will be necessary for students and their parents to keep up the pressure, but the proportion of professional educators ready to respond is high and from time to time the balance shifts in their favor. Thus it is that recent years have seen many stunning innovations in public schools: experimental "schools within schools," student participation in decision-making, use of the school itself as a laboratory for social and political studies, use of new kinds of reward systems for lower class children, field studies and work-study programs for high school students, involvement of people from the community—students, parents, citizens— as tutors and assistants to teachers, use of social scientists for crisis intervention and for training everybody connected with schools in crisis intervention, and so on (13).

Most of these innovations have not required any great pouring of money into the schools. Other reforms, such as better teacher training, better teacher-student ratios, and better facilities, particularly for ghetto schools, are, however, very expensive, and needed funds are not likely to be forthcoming until an aroused citizenry becomes actively aware of the crisis in education and is inspired by a new vision of education for democracy. Such awareness and inspiration is possible. In the city of Cleveland, Ohio, for example, a group of citizens committed themselves to share the blame for education in the urban setting, organized themselves as Programs for Action by Citizens in Education, and worked effectively in the role of a catalytic agent for change (14). This group saw clearly that it is up to our citizens to say what education in our society should be, and to provide a climate in which educators can do their work. But citizens and educators, however close their cooperation, can't do all that needs to be done. The problems, and the prospects, of the school call for all the moral and intellectual resources our society can muster.

All this will not meet the need, however, unless the effort is inspired by a rededication to the humanistic goals of education. There was a great upswing of public interest in education in the early 1960's and a great outlay of federal funds. Unfortunately this came at a time when national spokesmen for education were fascinated by a so-called "explosion in knowledge," and most educators, still defining their field as the learning of content, felt bound to use all possible means to speed the process. This opened the way for educational technologists who, with their "systems analysis" and "computerized instruction," not only left a trail of confusion and disappointment but contributed to the fragmentation and impersonality from which the schools suffer.

Once again, however, counterforces have been at work. Devotion to humanistic education has been persistent, though rarely dominant, in America, and this development has been strengthened by reaction to the new technological thrust. It appears, however, that many educators who favor liberating, or developmental, education have despaired of making progress within the public school system. Hence, there have been springing up around the country in recent years a large number of "experimental schools," "free schools," "in-community schools," and "after school schools." They are being started either by educators who have been "turned off" by the public school system or by educators with a special concern for young people who have been "turned off" by that system. These schools vary widely in philosophy and specific aims, but it is fair to say that all of them have conceptions of what young people need for their development and some kind of theory, however implicit, about how these needs are to be met by the new school's program. Soskin and Korchin, for example, started out with the aim of developing a therapeutic program for reducing "the incidence and prevalence of the use of hallucinogens and stimulants among high school and junior high school students." They are now operating a sort of "after-school school" which is the very model of a personality-developing institution. They write:

> The therapeutic program is designed to promote personal outcomes in these youth that will enhance ego development at this stage in the maturational process:
> 1. To improve their sense of self-identity
> 2. To promote a strong sense of personal competence
> 3. To effect a commitment to one's personal goals, to community, to one's fellow men. (15)

They are undertaking to improve these outcomes through a program embracing group therapy, seminars, small group activities, retreats, work projects, individual consultations, parent-youth consultations, and sessions with groups of parents—all designed in accord with hypotheses concerning ways in which these procedures work to promote development.

Soskin and Korchin note that the activities of their "place" are not ordinarily carried out in public schools and are not likely to be. They envision, therefore, the eventual institutionalization, with support by parents, of centers such as theirs.

Many of the new schools have been started with particular attention to the needs of ethnic minorities, and thus are a part of a movement to oppose those forms of legitimized evil which have as their effect the destruction of cultures. The black, brown, and red minority groups that seek to preserve, to reconstruct, and to build up their own cultures see that for reaching these goals the education of their children and youth is crucial. This education might well make use of the developmental approach being advocated here.

This approach to higher education has been the focus of much attention due to the efforts of minority groups to gain admission to college for higher proportions of their young people, and to institute ethnic studies programs and "Third World Colleges." Not only do these efforts put the student at the center of the educational enterprise, but the changes in admissions policy, in curriculum, in methods of teaching, and in the structure of institutions that are being urged would, if fully instituted, serve the needs of all students.

What these needs are and how they can be met in institutions of higher education make up the essential substance of the developmental approach to higher education. This approach has been the subject of an outpouring of literature in recent years. And the developmental approach is having a significant impact in practice. Numerous new programs, and some new institutions such as the Santa Cruz Campus of the University of California and Johnson College of the

University of Redlands, have been planned and set going largely in accord with it.

Once educators really accept the basic fact, now well established, that personality can and does develop during the college years, they have to ask how the various resources of the college may best serve developmental goals. They have to look at admissions with attention to various qualities and potentialities in addition to cognitive ability, at governance with attention to what forms best encourage the student to become his own authority, at the teaching of literature with a view to what methods favor growth in self-awareness, and so on for other educational policies, arrangements, and procedures.

Turning to widely agreed developmental goals such as independence of thinking—to name a trait that stands in direct opposition to authoritarianism—educators will see that practically all the college's resources can be brought into its service: not only governance that helps the student become his own authority and course content that helps him to become aware of his own impulses, but teaching that challenges preconceptions and gives practice in criticism, faculty members that serve as models of independent thinkers, and a general climate of freedom and respect for the individual.

This developmental approach to higher education is in its essentials the same as that advocated for child training in the home and for education in elementary and high schools. If we adopt this positive approach and become used to working within the framework it provides, the concept and the ideology of prevention will appear to be not only restricting but irrelevant. The aims of preventing specific evils are embraced by the larger aim of promoting human development, and preventive activities that do not keep this aim in view may actually set up barriers to its achievement. More, if we adopt the general theoretical approach advocated here but still cling to the idea of prevention, we will find ourselves speaking of preventing failures in development! It seems less awkward and, far more important, more stimulating, more hopeful, more worthy and, in the long run more practical, to be explicit about our aim of promoting development toward full humanity.

REFERENCES

1. HERSEY, J., *The Algiers Motel Incident*. New York: Knopf, 1968.
2. HAMMER, R., *One Morning in the Wars: The Tragedy at Son My*. New York: Coward-McCann, 1970; Hersh, S. M., *My Lai 4: A Report on the Massacre and its Aftermath*, New York: Random House, 1970.
3. SANFORD, N., COMSTOCK, C., and Associates, *Sanctions for Evil*. San Francisco: Jossey-Bass, 1971.
4. San Francisco Bulletin (c. 1860's): HEIZER, R., and ALMQUIST, A., *The Other Californians*, Berkeley: University of California Press, 1970; KROEBER, T., *ISHI*. University of California Press, 1961.
5. HERSEY, *op. cit.*
6. ARENDT, H., *Eichmann in Jerusalem*. New York: Viking Press, 1965.
7. FRIEDENBERG, E., Motown Justice. *New York Review of Books,* August 1968, 24-28.
8. BERNARD, V. W., OTTENBERG, P., REDL, F. Dehumanization: A Composite Psychological Defense in Relation to Modern War. In N. Sanford, C. Comstock, and Associates, *Sanctions for Evil*. San Francisco: Jossey-Bass, 1971.
9. *Ibid.,* p. 104.
10. BELLAH, R. Evil and the American ethos. In N. Sanford, C. Comstock, and Associates, *Sanctions for Evil.* San Francisco: Jossey-Bass, 1971.
11. ERIKSON, E. H. *Childhood and Society,* New York: W. W. Norton, 1950, Rev. Ed., 1964; WHITE, R. W. *Lives in Progress.* New York: Dryden, 1952; MASLOW, A. H. *Motivation and Personality.* New York: Harper and Row, 1954; BARRON, F. "What is Psychological Health," California Monthly, 1957, *68, 22-25;* ALLPORT, G. W. *Pattern and Growth in Personality.* New York: Holt, Rinehart and Winston, 1961.
12. ADORNO, T. W., FRENKEL-BRUNSWIK, ELSE, LEVINSON, D. J., and SANFORD, N., *The Authoritarian Personality.* New York: Harper and Row, 1950, p. 975.

13. For recent reports on these innovations see The Danforth Foundation and The Ford Foundation, *The School and the Democratic Environment*. New York: Columbia University Press, 1970; SILBERMAN, C. E. "Murder in the Schoolroom," Parts II and III, *The Atlantic Monthly*, 1970, 226, Nos. 1 and 2.

14. SMITH, W. L. "Cleveland's Experiment in Mutual Respect," in The Danforth Foundation and The Ford Foundation, *The School and the Democratic Environment*. New York, Columbia University Press, 1970, pp. 83-93.

15. SOSKIN, W., and KORCHIN, S. "Therapeutic Explorations with Adolescent Drug Users," Unpublished manuscript, Psychology Clinic, University of California, Berkeley, 1967.

4.

Anthropological Perspectives on Violence

WILTON S. DILLON, Ph.D.

In that mighty ocean (anthropology) anyone can catch a fish.

MARCEL MAUSS

Eᴿɪᴋ ʜ. ᴇʀɪᴋꜱᴏɴ (1), I trust, would agree that even the briefest of life histories or intellectual autobiographies might help provide a more realistic basis for objectivity. That is, it provides a clue to an author's biases, preferences, and selections. The observer is not an invisible man.

Unlike the post-Marcusean philosophers and activists who rationalize violence as a necessary means to noble ends —a changed social order—my peculiar dislike for violence grows out of several events of my own past. I grew up in cowboy and Indian country. A firsthand knowledge of American gun culture, whether oriented toward law and order, revenge killing, personal protection, or shooting rabbit and quail, is useful to understanding violence and its cultural roots. My earlier human environment provided much diversity, but what I strongly remember were chip-on-the-shoulder puritans, hospitable to strangers, yet quick to take slight and fight.

A move to the Deep South from Oklahoma frontier tradition found me living with my parents in Tuscaloosa where the local literati fed their creative imagination on such local color items as life at the national headquarters of the Ku Klux Klan, and the hanging in effigy of my heroine, Eleanor Roosevelt, at the University of Alabama. After a singularly unsuccessful military career during which I accidentally threw a live hand grenade at a tree under which stood my sadistic infantry captain (he had been unimpressed by my growling at a stuffed dummy in bayonet drill), I wound up as a civilian on General MacArthur's staff in Tokyo. My assignment: trying vainly to make millions of Japanese feel guilty for Japan's part in World War II. That is mainly how I became interested in anthropology; reading Ruth Benedict's *Chrysanthemum and the Sword* (2) gave me a framework for understanding important distinctions between shame and guilt, as well as Japanese notions of *giri* and *on* as background for Japan's extraordinary handling of their gift obligations, an interest in reciprocity which persists in my work to this day.

Later, in Berkeley as a student at the University of California, I helped to organize the Gandhi Memorial Library, and have made a pilgrimage to the scene of his earliest experiments with Satyagraha in South Africa. Then in recent years, six persons with whom I had enjoyed either friendship or personal conversation have died at the hands of assassins: the Kennedy brothers, Dr. Martin Luther King, Dr. Eduardo Mondlane of Mozambique, Sylvanus Olympio of Togo, and Tom Mboyo of Kenya. Though an Episcopalian, belonging to a milieu where military officers can feel quite comfortable and also get enshrined, I find myself on Quaker committees. Moreover, at the Smithsonian Institution, I am identified with a public effort to pool the insights of zoology, anthropology, and psychiatry to produce a symposium and now a book, *Man and Beast: Comparative Social Behavior* (3), a collective rejoinder to Dr. Konrad Lorenz and other scientists trying to figure out if and how aggression and violence are programmed into all animal behavior, including ours. Such are among the bits of background which undergird my intense personal interest in the subject, "Alternatives to Violence."

The widespread practice of mother-in-law avoidance behavior is the stuff of many an anthropologist's field notes, and a favorite theme of comedians and jokesters in various cultures (4). Adding to such classicism, I wish now to explore some possible preconditions for avoiding violence and encouraging harmony and competence. A more serious and "scientific" phrasing of my topic might be: "Structural and Psychological Pre-requisites of Violence-Avoidance Behavior." However, my sense of the absurd inhibits me from applying verbal rococo to such commonplace human inventions as mutual back-scratching, cheek-turning, and exchanging eyes for eyes and teeth for teeth.

In *Future Shock*, Alvin Toffler describes various kinds of "sensory shielding" we humans have employed to cut down levels of stimulation when our circuits become overloaded. "Don't bother me with new facts'" is a phrase usually uttered in jest, Toffler writes, adding that such a joke often disguises a real wish to avoid being pressed too hard by new data (5). Thus, in this essay, I will protect you from novelty, dealing instead with the mundane and the obvious: some already published and widely circulated excerpts from anthropological and related literature which illustrate mankind's vast cultural repertoire for moving toward violence, or away from it. Also, anecdotes from personal experience. Some ceremonies can function as kinds of cultural "psycho-dramas" to drain off rage. The only possible novelty I offer lies in a synthesis of a few theories and empirical materials to produce a diagnostic tool, or a social indicator of *potential* violence. Anthropologists and psychiatrists then can try out the tool in a variety of individual or collective situations, and perhaps design some models of human organization which will reduce or increase the chances for violence to spread within and between such human dyads or groups as lovers, families, clans, tribes, cities, or nation-states. At the end of this essay, you will have had the chance to re-confirm the truth of Edward Sapir's 1938 article, "Why Cultural Anthropology Needs the Psychiatrist" (6) .

The tool which I hope you psychiatrists, with your specialization in studying dependency, might help us anthropologists fashion would detect the stresses and strains between individuals or groups when donors and recipients fail to reverse their roles and, furthermore, fail to find exchange commodities to which both attach value. Frustrated gift behavior is neither necessary nor sufficient as an "explanation" for violence, but violence should not be a surprise when seen as a configuration of a multiple decline in one's sense of self-esteem, autonomy, initiative, and control over events.

Such a tentative probing for violence "readiness" or "proneness" grows out of the following generalizations from the work of Marcel Mauss, his 1927 essay, *The Gift: Form and Functions of Exchange in Archaic Societies* (7):

   1. Everything is stuff to be given away and repaid. Knowledge and intellectual goods are comparable

to tangible gifts. Literal or symmetrical quid pro quo is unnecessary to complete "closure" in a cycle of gift exchange.

2. The obligations to give, receive, and repay are interdependent. They are widely distributed in human societies in both time and space (e.g., the Samoans, the Maori, Andaman Islanders, New Caledonians, Trobrianders, Northwest Coast Indians in North America, the ancient Hebrews, Romans, Germans, and Hindus, and modern Japanese, French, Americans, and Chinese, among others).

3. People who give, desire something in return. People who receive, want to give something in return. Both are involved in the quest for reciprocity.

4. Conversely, the degree to which gifts are held with extreme suspicion as symbols of control (illustrated by "conflict of interest" concepts in American culture), suggests their power as an element in interpersonal relations.

5. The study of the concrete is the study of the whole.

Mauss (1872-1950), Emile Durkheim's nephew and most distinguished pupil, became the leading figure in French human sciences after Durkheim's death. His work continues to exercise an enormous influence on world anthropology through Claude Lévi-Strauss. His essay has stimulated me to bend my long-held interest in gift behavior, or reciprocity, in the direction of understanding its possible relationship to violence. Another vital source of inspiration is the work of Eliot D. Chapple on human interaction (8).

In *Gifts and Nations* (9), I used the words, "Gaullist effect" to refer to instances of human behavior when people take revenge on their benefactors. Such revenge is part of a search for reciprocity on the part of individuals or groups who feel obligated and dependent on others with no perceived way of alternating or reversing the roles of donor and recipient. Obligated people feel frustrated in their desire to "return the favor." Violence, verbal or physical, may serve as a form of counter-gift to redress the balance, providing "honor" to persons of lower rank or fewer resources who feel deprived of the status of donor or contributor. It is not more blessed to give than to receive, permanently.

"Societal arrangements," Maslow points out, "in themselves can either foster or discourage violence (10)."

In the simplest kind of war, such as a Riffian or Kentucky mountain feud, Chapple observed that origin of action must be balanced by origin of action, and crisis by crisis. "If we kill one of your group, you will not rest until you have killed one of ours, and only in one of the brief periods when the score is for the moment balanced can our two groups make peace," he and Coon wrote. They went on to mention the Ifugao of the Philippines where two groups may negotiate through an intermediary for an exchange of gifts and thus end the feud. "If they continue to exchange gifts at regular intervals, it will help build up a constant rate of interaction and establish an equilibrium between villages, making the outbreak of a second feud more difficult (11)."

Before introducing more ethnographic material to further suggest the interplay among obligations, hostility, and dependence as precursors to violence, and the role of gifts in peace-keeping, I should make a point about the difficulty of sticking to clear-cut definitions. I am tempted to use the filler found in contemporary speech, "You know," and let you attach your own meaning to these words.

Paraphrasing the New York subway ad, 'You don't have to be Jewish to like Levy's bread," I am finding, in a random sampling of literature on violence and non-violence, war and peace, hostility, frustration and aggression, that one does not have to be a Zen Buddhist to eschew dichotomies, to blur distinctions, or to embrace the notion of a seamless web. At first glance, the human condition might be described as yin-cum-yang and ping-cum-pong.

"War is not sharply distinguished from peace," the late Quincy Wright wrote (12), "Progress of war and peace between a pair of states may be represented by a curve: the curve descends toward war as tensions, military preparations, exchange of threats, mobilization, border hostilities, and limited hostilities culminate in total conflict; and it rises toward peace as tensions relax, arms budgets decline, disputes are settled, trade increases, and cooperative activities develop." Some students of warfare (Vayda, A. P.) (13) have put such labels on warfare as "animal," "primitive," or "civilized," and then others suggest what these disparate types have in common in trying to fit together their biological and social selves.

Research on nest-building behavior of the *quelea quelea* bird in Africa by the British zoologist, John H. Crook (14), stimulated, moreover, some interesting extrapolations involving sources of cooperation in human and other animals:

> Cooperation . . . is the collaborative behavior of two or more persons in the production of some common behavioral effect . . . some goal . . . in which there is common interest, emotional satisfaction or reward. . . . Human cooperation occurs at its most complex in the integrated work schedules of complex institutions—governments, universities, business firms, banks, ships—but also in the football match, in assistance given after a road accident, or in domestic washing up.

Citing caste and class distinctions and status hierarchy and other products of group and individual competition, Crook states:

> Both cooperation and competition exist together in any
> human organization; they are not simply the opposites
> of one another. Both belong to the same process. . . .
> Men, like monkeys, appear to cooperate best at their
> most competitive.

For psychiatrists accustomed to dealing with love-hate
combinations, talk of mergers of "opposites" is likely to pro-
voke the question, "So what's new?" That is what I am
trying to find out.

According to a recent conversation with Margaret Mead
(15), *violence refers to unsanctioned damage to persons or
property*. Warfare exists if the conflict is organized and socially sanctioned and killing is not regarded as murder. Good
old-fashioned traditional warfare such as World War I and
World War II failed to raise vexing questions of undeclared
wars. In more stylized wars, Geneva Convention style, rape
or looting after an armistice would be considered violence,
but warfare not. Similarly, capital punishment is outside such
a definition if it has the sanctions of a society operating
through the authority of the state. The Calley and Manson
cases dramatize the problem of both definition of violence
and its control. Whatever the definition, Harvey Wheeler
(16), the political scientist, reminds us that as an instrument
of social change, there is "good violence" and "bad violence."
And Hannah Arendt (17), citing Sorel, Pareto and Fanon,
provides a useful reminder that violence is neither "beastly
nor irrational," particularly in the minds of justice-minded
revolutionaries still caught up in the ends-means argument.
Arendt wrote: "The practice of violence, like all action,
changes the world, but the most probable change is to a
more violent world," spreading violence into the whole body
politic.

While seeing violence in the context of man's struggle to

adapt to his environment (the same can be said for magic, science, and religion), the dire implications of the contagion of violence are spelled out by the Stanford University psychiatrists who edited and wrote chapters in *Violence and the Struggle for Existence* (18), conceived in the wake of the assassination of Robert Kennedy. As an anthropologist, I invite psychiatrists to pursue with me the hunch that such contagion may be transmitted through bits of imitative behavior in various personal or international contexts. Behavior begets belief. The potentially dangerous upswing in the nuclear arms spiral, for example, represents the action-reaction phenomenon between the two super-powers imitating each other technologically and believing each other to be a menace. With less lethal weapons, the Chinese have now put a ball in President Nixon's corner of the ping-pong table and are awaiting another kind of action-reaction. (The June, 1971, decision to lift the U.S. trade embargo suggests that interactions starting with ping-pong have developed into a chain reaction, and that imitative behavior can work both ways on that spectrum Quincy Wright described between "war" and "peace.")

Allowing for such gradients in meaning, examination of Yanomamo culture in South America may reveal some significant clues about the strength of gift exchange as modifying, not eliminating, violence. Two villages feast, trade, find solidarity, and go off to raid and kill in another village. In the ethnographic film, *The Feast* (19), by Timothy Asch and Napoleon A. Chagnon, one can see evidence that would tempt cultural taxonomists to put the bellicose Yanomamo people at the opposite end of a scale on which we start with a model of violence-avoidance, say the Appolonian-style Pueblo Indians of Ruth Benedict's *Patterns of Culture* (20). Yet, even they seem capable of diversion from war, if not revenge raids, by the web of obligations developed through giving and receiving.

Chagnon (21) summarizes below certain aspects of his field work on the Yanomamo Indians who inhabit a humid tropical forest in southern Venezuela and adjacent portions of Brazil:

> Chronic warfare, and its associated ideals, permeate various aspects of Yanomamo culture.
>
> It may even be said that aggression is the theme of the Yanomamo way of life, the charter for which seems to lie in their myth about the Moon. The myth involves the tale of how the Moon, called Peribo, habitually visited earth to eat the souls of children between two pieces of cassava bread. Two brothers, Uhudima and Suhirina, took offense at Peribo's activities and decided to shoot him with their arrows. Uhudima tried first. But he was the poorer shot of the two brothers, and missed. Then, when Peribo reached his zenith, Suhirina shot one bamboo-tipped arrow into his abdomen, causing him to bleed profusely. Yeribo's blood spilled to earth and immediately changed into the first men (Yanomamo). It is because man came from the blood of Peribo that he is inherently fierce and wages constant war. Such is the explanation given by the Yanomamo . . . (who) . . . place a high value on bellicose behavior; all men are obliged to demonstrate their capacity to behave fiercely. . . . The propensity to display ferocity began early in the socialization process. Young boys are encouraged to strike their elders, then are rewarded for doing so with approving laughter by their parents. Girls, on the other hand, are taught to acquiesce timidly.

Chagnon, without alluding to Robert Ardrey's *Territorial Imperative,* insists that the Yanomamo militant ideology

and warfare represent no territorial gain as an objective (22).
He is equally unwilling to analyze Yanomamo agonistic
behavior according to the frustration-aggression hypothesis:

> Perhaps the tendency to dismiss non-territorial warfare
> with psychological explanations such as "release from
> pent-up emotions" or "expressing anger on outsiders to
> contribute to internal solidarity" have resulted from too
> few accurate descriptions of aboriginal warfare. . . . If
> warfare does release pent-up emotions of combatants,
> how do we account for the frustrations in the first
> place? . . .

While Chagnon finds some answers to that question in
cultural ecology (the interaction between the tribal center
and the tribal periphery and the relationship of both to neighboring, hostile villages), he points out, significantly, that
trading, feasting, and alliances are important factors in
handling ecologically-induced hostility and aggression; allied
villages are expected to give refuge to each other in times
of need. Only revenge raids disturb such alliances. Allies confront each other boastfully and demonstrate that they do not
require assistance and probably never will, for the obverse
implication is that they are weak and can be exploited by
a stronger group (23).
He continues:

> Were it not for the fact, recognized by all Yanomamo
> but rarely discussed, that no village can exist indefi-
> nitely without friendly allies, the Yanomamo would
> probably have very little inter-village contact. This
> paradoxical set of attitudes—allies need each other but
> refuse to acknowledge it overtly—has given rise to a
> peculiar relationship between economic specialization,
> trade, and alliance.

In daily gift behavior, an individual will give a particular item, a dog, for example, to a friend in an allied village, saying: "I give you this dog, *no mraiha*." Superficially, the *no mraiha* looks like a free gift, since the recipient does not give anything in return at that time. But *no mraiha* "gifts" are not free presentations: each object must be repaid at a later time with a different kind of article, i.e., it is reciprocating trade of the kind described by Mauss in *The Gift*. Thus each trade calls forth another, a type of deficit spending that insures peaceful, frequent inter-village visiting. Trade is the first step in a possible more intimate social relationship: inter-village feasting . . . which carries with it more obligations and implies therefore a greater degree of solidarity . . . promotes a good deal of cooperation . . . and generates a high-level of enthusiasm and excitement that is carried over to the feast (24) .

Shifting from South America to the Pacific, I want to mention now another charming group of people, the Dobu islanders off the coast of New Guinea. These former cannibals may be as well known already to anthropologized psychiatrists as are Freud's famous cases, but they deserve a new look. They help us to focus on the capacity of some cultures to combine, through gift exchange, a hostile and violent domestic way of life with a "peaceful" set of reciprocal trade and gift relations with strangers.

Though Malinowski found these dark-skinned, big-headed, round-shouldered, gnome-like people "definitely pleasant, honest and open . . . general favorites of the whites . . . the best and most reliable servants" (25) , they are also characterized in Reo Fortune's *The Sorcerers of Dobu* (1932) and Ruth Benedict's *Patterns of Culture* (20) as dangerous magician-warriors who put a premium upon ill will and treachery and make of them the recognized virtues of their society. Adultery is a favorite pastime. Children are bribed to spy on adulterous parents, their tenuous relationship strained even further by quarrels over hereditary proprietorship of yam-producing gardens and the quest for magical formulae. All existence is cut-throat competition, and every advantage is gained at the expense of a defeated rival. Disease-causing charms are placed on goods or trees as claims to property. Suspicion runs to paranoid lengths.

But like the Yanomamo, the Dobu have a penchant for gift exchange with outsiders. They share with other Melanesians a passion for endless reciprocal transactions, ideally passing goods through each man's hands without keeping them as permanent possessions. The famous institution invented to satisfy such needs is the Kula ring, a system of international exchange including a dozen islands lying in a circle 150 miles in diameter. Described in great detail in Dr. Malinowski's *Argonauts of the Western Pacific* (25), and used by me in *Gifts and Nations* (9) as a counterpoint to my study of the Marshall Plan, the Kula ring brings enormously different cultures, with contrasting motivations, into peaceful intercourse with each other. The Kula ring is a circle of islands around which one kind of valuable travels in one direction and another in the other in semi-annual exchange. In canoes, men of each island make long sea voyages to carry shell necklaces in clockwise direction and counterclockwise for armshells. Each man has his partner in the exchanging Island and bargains for advantage by every means at his control. Local specialization of industry encourages such exchanges, for one people polishes greenstone, another makes canoes, and another pottery. The Trobrianders, who trade with Dobuans and others, differ sharply in their cultural ethos, having a chiefly aristocracy, whereas the Dobu lack chiefs and show marked deference to others based on rank. Dobus mark their return from Kula exchanges by stressing to the home folk their own gains at the expense of another's loss. Trobrianders come home to the pleasures of cooperative work valued in itself, aesthetically polishing their gardens, and studiously balancing in their social life a complex set of traditional forces, duties, and obligations.

The ceremonial aspects of the exchange, however, serve to put these cultural differences in perspective: one transaction does not finish the Kula relationship. A partnership between two men is a permanent and lifelong affair. These relationships are reinforced in the Kula by being rooted in myth, backed by traditional law, and surrounded by magical rites in public ceremonies which follow definite procedures. The credit arrangements imply a high degree of mutual trust. These linguistically, racially and' culturally different Pacific islanders, in the context of the Kula ring, operate in a kind of third culture common to the participants. The participants seem, therefore, to represent a capacity to live bi-culturally, alternating different life styles at home and abroad, and most importantly for my crude argument, also alternating their roles as donors and recipients. Such violence-avoidance behavior might have occurred internationally, or intertribally, without the Kula invention. Yet, my suspicion is that nothing is so effective for satisfying both social and material needs as gift exchange relationships on the Kula model. My aim is to speculate how the Kula characteristics might be built into relationships between and within nation-states as the most violence-prone conglomerations operating on the earth's surface today.

Anthropologists and psychiatrists might form their own Kula to explore my earlier point: we need a better detection system for stresses and strains between individuals and groups when donors and recipients fail to reverse their roles, and furthermore fail to find exchange commodities to which both attach value.

An empirical starting point is my own study of stresses

and strains within the Atlantic alliance during the period of European recovery from the ravages of World War II. I shall not repeat here, except in broadest outline, the hunches and data expressed in *Gifts and Nations* (9). I became particularly interested in French relations to American generosity and protection during the Marshall Plan. I have already mentioned "the Gaullist effect" as revenge against such philanthropy. Well-intentioned Americans failed to stress their enlightened self-interest as donors, and failed, in addition, to cushion the recipients from the demoralizing shock of having their historic role as teacher-donor reversed to that of pupil-recipient. We felt an obligation to give. The French felt the obligation to receive, for they needed help (remember the Yanomamo reluctance to admit such needs without a big ceremony to cover up such admissions?). Both were uneasy about how to deal with the third obligation: the obligation to repay. The tensions rising out of the ambiguity surrounding that obligation were not easily dissipated by NATO rhetoric about a common Russian enemy and the economic undergirding Western democratic allies might require as immunity from the appeals of communism. The French felt squeezed between two giants. The return of heroic Charles de Gaulle to the political scene had the psychological impact in France of reducing dependence and increasing self-esteem vis-à-vis the United States, and providing, moreover, a gift to the U.S.—showing the Russians that France, the original protector of Western civilization, could set a good example for East European satellites of the USSR by rising up and practicing self-determination right within "the Western bloc" controlled by the United States. General de Gaulle's tactics were not those of Gandhi, nor of the Hungarians, but the history of his rule deserves study for the light it might shed on how nation-states, like individuals, seek autonomy by getting rid of obligations which seem unbearable. Studying

French culture in the tribal sense, as an integrated whole, is comparable to peeling an onion. I found a remarkable consistency between the gift behavior of individuals and families on one hand, and the head of state who symbolized and acted out, on a larger stage, their own highly institutionalized and patterned values about reciprocity. That the "father-figure" was finally "killed off" does not mean that French reciprocity patterns dissolved, and were buried with de Gaulle at Colombey des Deux Eglises.

How does violence-avoidance fit in here as a concept? If we used Margaret Mead's definition of violence as unsanctioned damage to persons or property, one can think like a lawyer and deal with intent or motive to "commit violence," or like an anthropologist and take note of verbal violence and passive resistance as indicators that dissonance has set in, that the rhythms of giving and receiving are fouled up, and that physical violence might pop up in some other context, not aimed directly at the source of frustration.

Simple peoples, civilized peoples, mild peoples, and violent, assertive peoples will all go to war if they have the invention of war, Mead has pointed out, adding that a people can use only the forms it has. This statement could be paraphrased to refer to the behavior of individuals or to nations' responses to unrequited obligations to reciprocate. If they cannot offer gifts which they and the original donor value, they will take dramatic, *unauthorized* action to provide some kind of attention-getting feedback, even revenge, in order to escape the feelings of being indebted, supervised, protected, and controlled. Without a mechanism for giving what they valued, they have to invent (what at the Smithsonian is called a "short-lived phenomenon") a cathartic happening to pursue self-interest or regain self-respect.

Witness the events of July, 1956, when the late President Nasser nationalized Suez. Dark feelings developed between

France, Britain, and the United States on how to deal with
Egypt. By Halloween Week of that year, the Atlantic Alliance had nearly collapsed. Eden, Pineau, and Mollet were
much in the news. American ships were poised to prevent by
force British and French efforts to take a military promenade
with Israel into Egypt to avenge Nasser's action. Secretary
of State John Foster Dulles called in the French Ambassador,
Hervé Alphand, and, according to the Alsop brothers, writing
on November 3 that year, "gave him the kind of lecture that
an old-fashioned school master might give to a juvenile delin-
quent." James Reston, reporting to the *New York Times*
from Washington the same day, wrote: 'So sharp and strong
were the feelings here about the British-French policy of
force that the crisis in the Western alliance over-shadowed
even the grave events of the Middle East." And a less pub-
licized but psychologically significant response came from
Florida on November 2 where General James Van Fleet,
former U.N. commander in Korea, charged that the action
of Britain, France, and Israel was "the meanest thing any
ally who has received our money could possibly do to Uncle
Sam."

Our allies deliberately withheld prior consultations about
their actions, or even reporting in advance their decision to
use force against Nasser. Their "secret" plans to invade
Egypt were a climax to at least five years of mounting ambivalence toward U.S. generosity, advice, and protection.
Like the well-meaning parents whose children run away
from home because of too much loving supervision, or the
school teacher who sees her star pupils crawl out of the
window to play hooky, we stood hurt, feeling isolated, charg-
ing "collusion" and "trickery" and reproaching our allies for
lack of gratitude "after all we have done."

Some French intellectuals perceived the Marshall Plan
as an enormous potlatch ceremony which, like the Kwakiutl

Indians' invention, served to humiliate the guests who were
not wealthy enough to burn up their blankets and coppers.
A French anthropologist, while agreeing that the reactions
of many of his countrymen represented non-rational fears
about becoming an American colony, especially so soon after
the Germans had left, remembered another "primitive" custom besides the Kwakiutl potlatch. He knew of Professor
Douglas Oliver's work at Harvard on the Solomon Island
villages of the Siuai people where men of high socio-political
rank give presents of pigs and money in order to humiliate
others. The Solomon donors give purposefully to create un-
fulfillable obligations hoping that their gifts will not be
returned (26). We seemed more like the Siuai than the
participants in a Kula ring.

In the French business community which had been on
the front line of interaction with the American managerial
class during the Marshall Plan and was shocked at our
indifference to French know-how, I found the following
testimony in an interview in a small factory outside Paris
(27). I shall call the industrialist Monsieur Bernard. He took
the role of professor, and I was cast as pupil.

"You Americans understand very little about the psychology of Islam," he started. "As people in your government probably have never read the Koran, they don't know
how quickly Moslems will be able to submit to Communist
authority. A *marabou* can easily become a *commissar*."

Monsieur Bernard seemed to feel this was his patriotic
duty to say this—and more—to any American who would
listen. As a man who confessed to learning a lot about
running a factory from Americans during the Marshall Plan,
he wanted to pay back his obligations with gifts in the form
of political education.

The Suez crisis was in one of its various boiling points
as he spoke. The users association had just been proposed.

A month earlier, he had closed his plant, cut off his mail, and fled the world of newspapers and telephones to sail around Corsica for his August vacation. Upon return, he was enraged to read in his *Figaro* that the U.S. was keeping France from "stopping the new Hitler in Cairo."

"If there is anything I can do to pay back America for her generosity to France, and for all I learned there, I want to prepare you to go home to tell other Americans what they don't know, or care to understand about the Moslems." He seemed pleased that I was copying this in my notebook, and continued.

"Allah respects strong men. America has made herself, Britain and France —the entire Occident—look weak in the eyes of Nasser. And it's all the worse because Nasser takes comfort by knowing it was Roosevelt who told the Sultan of Morocco the U.S. would help get the French out of North Africa." Bernard, to prove his point, took down from his book-shelf a copy of Elliot Roosevelt's *As He Saw It*. Red pencil marks underlined the paragraph stating what Elliot heard his father tell the Sultan in 1943 about a promise for American moral support against colonial rule. The book was worn for having been circulated among relatives and business frends of Monsieur Bernard.

Bernard was not interested in partisan politics in America. The doctrinal lines between the Republicans and the Democrats seemed too fuzzy. What was clear to him, as a French bourgeois and patriot, was that Roosevelt seemed the devil who undermined French prestige by whispering in Arab ears. On the other hand, Truman was the triumphant angel who could act with the strength and passion that Moslems could understand. That Roosevelt and Truman were Democrats was, to him, beside the point.

"Roosevelt was dangerous because he was an idealist, and knew the power of words," he told me. "Truman was more like a Frenchman—a realist—when he sent troops into Korea; just as we should be doing in Egypt right now."

"What about Eisenhower," I asked. "He's a good soldier, but since the time he left France in 1963, he doesn't seem to know what's been going on here . . . if he had remembered his lessons from the time he spent in North Africa during the war, he should have ordered Foster Dulles to read the Koran every morning. . . . Americans might then have been influenced to realize that Allah loves strong men, and now only Russia looks strong to the Moslems."

Monsieur Bernard wrote me from Paris to New York later that year to say that the United States ought to share atomic knowledge with France, and enlarge the exclusive Anglo-Saxon club which then cut out the French, but not the British, from certain kinds of atomic research. We were not completely generous, and were too selective with our gifts, he charged. Scientists throughout the whole Occident needed to be abreast of atomic energy in order to meet the "Communist threat." Back in Paris on December 9, 1958, I interviewed Monsieur Bernard again to find him jubilant over de Gaulle's return to power. The U.S., he told me, will now have to deal with France as an equal partner, especially now that France, once refused atomic secrets, had decided to go ahead with research on an atomic bomb.

On February 13, 1960, the French exploded an atomic device over the Sahara. This served to outrage black Africans, especially Nigerians, who broke diplomatic ties with France. Our response to the whole affair was unenthusiastic, and we began to lump the French with the Chinese, who were having similar problems getting information from the Russians, and were evolving similar attitudes toward a nuclear test-ban treaty, i.e., opposing it.

The desire of Washington to prevent the proliferation of atomic weapons makes good sense here as defense strategy.

But France would not have been so insistent on having the bomb, I suspect, if: (a) we had admitted our historic debt to French research (well known in the DuPont labs in Wilmington), or (b) if we had not acted as though we thought the French were incapable of making atomic weapons. The bomb tests in the Sahara were, of course, logical extensions of de Gaulle's quest for France's return to big power status. They also can be interpreted as an act of "revenge" against the United States for alleged treatment of the French as children not intelligent enough to make dangerous toys, nor responsible enough to play with those of American manufacture.

In Africa later, amidst African demonstrations against French "pollution of the African earth" by the bomb tests, and against "America's NATO ally who wants to poison the air breathed by the black man," I tried to suggest that the French were really more interested in proving themselves to the Americans and themselves, as a defiance against American "rule," than they were indifferent to blacks who have, after all, not suffered from the color bar in French colonies. The Africans did not buy my nice little theory of French atomic grandeur, and felt no identity with the French then as soul brothers in a common fight against the dependency of colonialism in old or new forms. Still, I found the twin gifts of protection and supervision were no more appreciated in Europe than in Africa.

It was no surprise to me to read that Francois de Rose of the French Institute of Strategic Studies agreed with McGeorge Bundy in a Copenhagen speech in which Bundy declared: "The problem of defense in the nuclear age is as much psychological as military." To that I would add: the handling of obligations by people and nations of differing cultures is part of the stuff of the "psychological problem." McGeorge Bundy made his statement without knowing that my informant, Monsieur Bernard, while accusing the U.S. of jealousy over French success with the bomb, can be moved to appreciative tears over the sight of American graves at Verdun, or the sight of Americans placing wreaths at statues of LaFayette.

Annoying as these relationships have been for the past decade or so, the Franco-American ties remain deeply familial, the kinds of spats one has among kin and intimates, bearing little resemblance to the chasms now separating the Russians from their Chinese comrades. Shared suffering, remembered along with past arguments, gives a family license to take verbal liberties with each other. With such liberties, the French can better us; their verbal weapons help them adapt to an unreciprocal environment. Words are important elements of violence-avoidance behavior. It is interesting to look at those strains within the Atlantic Alliance in the light of generalizations of Triandis and Lambert in "Sources of Frustration and Targets of Aggression." "In general there may be no strong relationship between sources of frustrations and targets of aggression. . . ." However, they suggest that societies with much in-group verbal aggression are consistently less likely to engage in other kinds of aggression (28).

Herman Melville's famous words he wrote as dialogue for Billy Budd are pertinent here: "Could I have used my tongue I would not have struck him." To which Captain Vere replied: "Struck dead by an angel of God. Yet the angel must hang." Reciprocity?

Still in search of some of the basic principles of the Kula ring that might be built into external relations of nation-states, I think it important to examine transactions and reciprocal behavior within such states. In *Gifts and Nations* (9), I recommended that research workers and policy philosophers pay attention to the domestic ways of handling reciprocity. A significant response to this suggestion has come from Dr. Robert Pruger of the School of Social Welfare at the University of California, Berkeley. His unpublished book, *Reciprocity and the Poor*, picks up where I left off in my book. Using Mauss' three obligations—to give, receive, and repay—Pruger examines welfare problems on the home front, and finds confusion relating to all three.

On April 26, President Nixon, in his speech before the U.S. Chamber of Commerce, showed clear signs that Pruger's and my messages still deserve a hearing, banal and obvious as they may seem. President Nixon, though correct about welfare being demeaning, declared:

> We need to take a lot more pride in the system (private enterprise) that makes it possible for us to be the most generous and compassionate nation on the face of the earth. . . . You can be confident that certain American values are not going to change. *One of these values is compassion for the dependent. Another of these values is the dignity of work.* (Emphasis mine.) The able-bodied people who think they can take a free ride are just going to have to get out and push with the rest of us.

These words suggest that the President and his welfare advisors, and indeed welfare recipients themselves, have not been able to articulate yet the basis of a social contract around which people who receive welfare raised from taxes can be reminded of their obligations to return the favor with contributions to the welfare of the society as a whole. The rhetoric usually stops just at a call for self-help, with an innuendo about laziness, and does not encourage exploitation of the poor as contributors to the quality of the whole. Pride in being compassionate for the dependent without a suggestion for how that dependency can end, except work for the sake of work, seems to smack of the same paternalism that served the U.S. so poorly vis-à-vis foreign aid and the outside world. Eleanor Roosevelt repeatedly reminded us that Americas' greatest weakness was our complacency about what other people had to offer,

In a position paper prepared for the platform committees of the Democrats and Republicans during the last presidential campaign, I amplified some of these points. How may these be improved in the next go-round? In reading the statement reproduced below, remember that it was written before James Forman had demanded cash reparations from white churches for white injustices to blacks, and also before the aerospace industry crisis left numerous professional whites in the ranks of unemployed welfare cases. Yet would psychiatrists agree that the major points are still valid?

ON DESIGNING A DOMESTIC MARSHALL PLAN

Vice-President Hubert Humphrey's second call for an urban "Marshall Plan" for rebuilding America's cities ought to inspire men and women of all parties to look carefully at what was wrong psychologically with the original Marshall Plan before uncritically using it as a model to increase the chances for disadvantaged cities, and people, in our society. We need to learn some lessons from our foreign aid that can be applied at home.

Western Europe did make, thanks in part to our recovery plan, a remarkable economic comeback. Yet our cold war philanthropy prevented the development of any effective reciprocity between the United States and our then European "welfare cases." We gave generously without stating our national self-interest, enlightened or otherwise. We failed to ask for, in return for Marshall Plan help, the benefits of European science and technology, geopolitical advice, and other ideas to which the recipients attached value.

European nations, especially France, found no way

to discharge the obligations they felt, and we did not ask their help. Instead, we expected gratitude anti-Communist votes, and permission to station troops. We also enjoyed watching Europeans switch toward mass production and mass consumption, i.e., becoming more like us.

With what result? The most extreme form of "backlash" against our benevolent hcgcmony is what might be called "the Gaullist effect"—the quest for self-esteem, initiative and autonomy which sets in when recipients seek revenge against benefactors who confuse gifts with bribes, and do not know how to attach the right strings.

(The French apparently grumbled more than the British who, after all, had not been so demoralized by defeat and occupation. They had already enjoyed a pleasant lend-lease relationship with us during World War II, and they have a particular knack for thinking up appropriate gifts: Marshall Fellowships for American students to study in Britain, or a piece of cherished Magna Carta territory in memory of John F. Kennedy.)

Perhaps Mr. Humphrey's proposed National Urban Development Bank will enjoy the built-in safeguards of interest rates which will allow cities and their poor people to give something in return to the whole nation. Thus the plan could ward off the evil spirits which spring out of lordly giving and obsequious receiving. The urban bankers and lenders may also benefit from the sophisticated administrators of the Office of Economic Opportunity, who know that social unrest does not disappear with money. They also know by now that social calm and orderly progress do not set in automatically when "the poor" are invited to participate in planning programs for their own, and everybody's, good.

Racial questions were absent from the Marshall Plan. Black, white, red and yellow Americans were help-

ing their white European brothers. It is a different story
when it comes to designing a domestic Marshall Plan
aimed at rebuilding cities with highly visible black people in the middle of them. The urban poor, regardless of
color, are not unlike the Europeans of the Marshall
Plan period who had strongly mixed feelings about being helped. Self-pity, coupled with few chances to feel
worthy enough to "make a contribution," breeds hostility against helpers. And helpers become hostile against
the ungrateful helped, thus starting a vicious circle of
unproductive distrust.

Self-pity and ambivalent demands for help in exchange for past injustices are not to disappear through
mea culpa litanies of "white racism" as the causes of
violence in cities. Trying to make whites feel guilty for
"racism" or blacks feel guilty for rioting and looting is
a dangerous tactic. A new Marshall Plan should spell out
everybody's civic duty. It should state the national rewards for getting rid of prejudice and the economic
barriers to human development. It could even adopt
as its motto that line from the Kennedy inaugural about
what you can do for your country.

The rioting of 'ghetto" dwellers in 164 U.S. commu-
nities during the summer of 1967 produced the first call
for a domestic Marshall Plan. No doubt the riots after
the murder of Martin Luther King, and the poor people's
campaign in Washington in June, 1968, helped to prompt
Mr. Humphrey's second call. After both waves of riots,
the rioters were charged with ingratitude because they
felt no obligation to be thankful—either for civil rights
legislation, court decisions, or public investment in
urban renewal and slum clearances of earlier years. The
National Advisory Commission on Civil Disorders in
1968 called for a "compassionate, massive and sustained
national action to prevent America from becoming two
societies, one black, one white, separate and unequal."

The word "compassionate" is significant. It suggests one-way giving.

The report recognized what John W. Gardner of the Urban Coalition and Wilbur Cohen, his successor in the cabinet, well understand: the demoralizing effect of welfare, and recommended the creation of 550,000 jobs and 500,000 housing units. Scant attention was given to what impoverished blacks, or poor whites, might contribute to the national welfare in the way of talent, skilled manpower, or ultimate purchasing power. No reference was made to the cultural diversity of American Indians, blacks, Spanish-speaking Americans or Anglo-Saxon mountaineers and other ethnic minorities without whose different life styles American civilization would lack zest and be left saddled with an outmoded and unworkable theory of the melting pot.

Black and white spokesmen concentrated on historic wrongs and injustices. *Life* magazine's March 8, 1968, issue on "The Negro and the Cities" featured a cover picture of a weeping black child with the caption, "the cry that will be heard." Gordon Parks' text evoked pathos: "Try to understand my struggle against your racism." This has been the plea, too, of Sen. Fred R. Harris of Oklahoma who has asked Rep. Hale Boggs of Louisiana to list "white racism" as a cause of violence when Boggs' Democratic party platform committee starts its drafting at the Chicago convention. (While such confessions make some blacks and whites feel better, I am reminded that our Marshall Plan clients in Europe took similar but inconsequential pleasure in hearing affluent American intellectuals and moralists attack U.S. "materialism.")

The designers of a new Marshall Plan might well go beyond this point and, admitting that we have all been bad, commission such students of human resources as John Hope II to bring up to date Eli Ginzberg's *The*

Negro Potential. Some Black Power militants have told me they prefer a tough-minded, unsentimental development-of-talent approach to that of the innocent paternalism of white liberals who "want to help" and expect nothing in return.

The best-intentioned public servants, editors of the mass media, and legislators seem innocent about the hazards of charity, pity and guilt. Unless accompanied by an attitude that the recipient has something to offer, that he dislikes being on a permanent dole, the "donors" —the more affluent majority acting through public officials—court new opportunities for social conflict when they act benevolently and then expect, in return, gratitude and docility.

Theologians and the clergy who march for the poor need to give some fresh attention to the proposition that mercy exalts the free gift. It should be revised to include a religious obligation to demand that all of God's creatures, rich and poor, exploit each others' minds, talents and skills. We need more than compassion on a one-way direction and a political theory of gifts and obligations which could guide both the majority and minority toward a more palatable form of social contract, free from backlashes of various colors. Otherwise, we face a new wave of "Gaullist effect"—black, beige, red and white—crashing against our newest efforts to launch a domestic Marshall Plan.

One of the superficial troubles with my propositions is found in the lag, the sluggish or begrudging response on the part of the angry "dependents" when efforts are made to stimulate a reversal of the role of the recipient to that of a contributor to the national welfare. It takes more than exhortation to change a self-image. Indeed, we need structural and economic changes, and educational messages internalized, before a general sense of meaning and worthiness can be found for individuals caught in what Oscar Lewis called the "culture of poverty." It is easier to shout about rights to "life, liberty, and pursuit of happiness" and to demand reparations for past injustices than to become a gift-bearing citizen with the incipient characteristics of a Rotarian or Optimist. Margaret Mead found this out in a 1971 speech in Washington before a gathering of American Indians. She reminded them that Indian traditions in the United States, despite much cultural decimation, carried with it some valuable wisdom and techniques of re-cycling, for example, for use in the ecology movement, and the international concern growing over the crisis of quality in the planetary environment. Some Indians and their pale-face protectors angrily replied: "What have they, the majority, done to deserve Indians' help?" That was a predictable first response: disbelief that there could be another set of expectations than those they had long adapted to. Nevertheless, these three little Indian stories will suggest, in a microcosmic way, how the dependency role can alternate with that of the citizen-contributor:

(1) The San Carlos Apache Indians in Arizona offered a three-day feast and ceremonial to a Ghanaian poultry husbandryman I sent to study their methods of managing cooperatives for marketing cattle; they had never been asked to do anything for American "foreign aid," and begged to be of further service;

(2) At the Westward Ho Hotel in Phoenix, Dr. Karl Menninger was scheduled to be the principal speaker at a luncheon held at the meetings of the National Congress of American Indians. He rose to speak, and said, "I am here to give you a big listen." He sat down. The astonished Indians showed various kinds of culturally-determined signs of pleasure: ranging from applause, to

silent nods of approval. Department of the Interior officials cannot be expected to behave like a psychiatrist, the professional listener *par excellence,* but Dr. Menninger made his symbolic gesture, and now Indians like Vine DeLoria are picking up the opportunity, and writing and talking (29);

(3) I once accompanied an African, a Kikuyu tribesman to the rose garden at the White House with a group of American Indian tribal officials for a ceremonial audience with John Kennedy. (He was writing a Ph.D. dissertation on American tribalism, or what in Africa used to be called "native administration.") Characteristically, President Kennedy refused the Indians' gift of a plumed war bonnet (he did not wear hats), earning his right to solicit on the spot a gift to which he attached great value: their votes. Subsequent events, symbolized by "Red Power" slogans and Alcatraz suggest that Indians also value voting along with other kinds of social action.

Mauss said that the theme of the gift, of freedom and obligation in the gift, of generosity and self-interest in giving, reappear in society like the resurrection of a dominant motif long forgotten. But a mere statement of what is taking place is not enough. We should deduce from it some course of action or moral precept.

Having glimpsed at excerpts from anthropological literature or direct experience, from the various cultural settings —South America, the Pacific, Euro-America, and the Atlantic basin— (I haven't even touched on the rich material I could produce from my field work in Africa), or youth culture and the conflict of generations. I wish to end this paper by repeating my hope stated at the start: that psychiatrists and anthropologists, might try making our own Kula ring, to design some models of human organization which will reduce or increase the chance for violence to spread within and between such human dyads or groups as lovers, families, clans, tribes, cities, or nation-states. Regardless of the scale of organization or community, I propose that we search for operational meanings to these three prescriptions, trying them out at various places in the concentric circles as we move from small groups to nation-states and global society or world village:

I. LEADERSHIP AS A FORM OF INVITING GIFTS

Leadership, practiced by individuals and nations, consists of discovering the means by which individuals or nations feel indebted, and after discovering their potential gifts, asking them to offer their gifts toward a common goal or common good. Recognition of positions of leadership is found in the willingness of followers to accept what the donor-leader-teacher thinks are the proper gifts to offer a joint enterprise. The giving and use of such gifts constitutes a specialization or role differentiation within the group. Thus gift exchange can be a form of dividing labor and utilizing human potentials, and contribute to the reduction of potential violence.

II. THE IMPORTANCE OF FUNCTIONAL RECIPROCITY IN HUMAN ORGANIZATION

Recognizing that knowledge of human and animal behavior can be applied to both peace and war, a major task of peace-loving anthropologists, psychiatrists, and political leaders is to invent designs of human organization based upon the principle of functional reciprocity. Such designs would take into account the need for well-balanced chains of reciprocal services. Hostility and tension would be like elements in the balancing process as there are always problems of allocation and coordination of balance between the parts. The making of gifts and the delivery of return gifts would be among the ways of organizing an equilibrium and the building of a common culture with full recognition of the values of diversity.

III. *THE IMPORTANCE OF PLAY, HUMOR, AND CEREMONY IN HUMAN INTERACTION*

Recognizing that science and art themselves are probably derived from "the play impulse" in mammals, that laughter, wit, and humor can be both tension-producing—in the case of ridicule— or tension-releasing, and that these can all be incorporated into a system of gift exchange, we need to build into our model the positive elements of surprise, caprice, the mysterious, the sacred, and the ceremonial. For modern man, despite his legalisms and literal-mindedness, can live a richer, fuller and more finely textured life by a mixture of the rational and non-rational, and the sharing of sets of changing symbols.

The Irish wit and polemicist friend of mine, Dr. Conor Cruise O'Brien, now a member of the volatile Irish Parliament, and the bearer of wounds from street violence in New York and Belfast, a culture carrier of both Quakerism and Roman Catholicism, has written a book, *The United Nations: Sacred Drama* (30), an allegedly libelous morality play about Hammarskjold, *"Murderous Angels,"* and a recent essay for the Smithsonian, *"Actors, Roles and Stages,"* which is about politics as theater. In this, the 25th year of the United Nations, these are the closest analogies we have

to the Kula ring, or the old Iroquois confederacy, I propose
that we solicit the wit and wisdom of even the violence-
prone Irish, and work on some scenarios for quickening the
sense of theater at the United Nations (31). If we cannot
expect the Yanamamo to show us how to lay on a feast in
the Security Council, in New York, we might ask U. Thant
or Dr. Cruise O'Brien to beg the Chinese to let the UN
hold its next session in the Forbidden Palace in Peking.
Chiang Kai Shek could be invited to lend his favorite chefs
and Sung porcelains for the banquet; the Russians could
read poetry, and the various kinds of Indo-Chinese, introduced by Vice-President Agnew, could dance out the myths
of Angkor-Wat. There could even be a ballet replay of the
scene (now instant tradition) in Peking when Glenn Cowan
and other American pingpong players walked on to the
stadium floor to banners and applause. Cowan, clad in a tie-
dye purple bell-bottoms, at a loss over how to reciprocate,
broke into a sort of frug to the strains of a somewhat unfamiliar tune: Sailing the Seas Depends on the Helmsman,
Making Revolution Depends on Mao Tse-Tung's Thought.
We could also light eternal flames for the dead in all wars,
with a special candle for Charles de Gaulle.

Less fanciful but real was this conversation I had at a
recent Princeton conference on "The United Nations, Its
Future, the World Environment, and U.S. Foreign Policy."
An American diplomat had just asserted that the U.S. was
more interested than the Russians in yielding to UN peace-
keeping machinery. A Russian diplomat had complained
that this was not so. To hear out the Russian's views in more
detail, I followed him and two companions to lunch. One
of the other Russians was introduced to me as their ecology
man, "In preparation for the Stockholm conference, we call
him Mr. Environment." "You mean Mr. Clean?" I asked.
Laughter followed, and he was dubbed "Mr. Clean" by the
Russians for the rest of the conference. I then told him that

an anthropologist was making a study of the ecology movement as a new religion. The first Russian appeared surprised,
and quickly replied: "If you Americans are plotting to
encourage such a religion, move it into the United Nations,
and turn the UN into a church, then you can expect it will
give us some profound ideological problems." More laughter.

Where do anthropologists and psychiatrists go from
here? What have we to contribute jointly and separately to
understanding violence and its avoidance? How can we move
from clinical experience and case studies to understanding
unsanctioned damage in larger human groups, ranging from
street gangs, to nation-states? This essay can only raise these
questions, and provide some glimpses of the possibilities of
our joint enterprise. A science of human behavior must rest
on a broad cross-cultural perspective (32), as well as on the
specificity of individual psyches with records of childhood
experience. So let us start by exchanging gifts with each
other now, and recognizing that verbal violence may be a
sign of intimacy, of showing that we care for each other,
and that harmonious agreement may be hazardous to truth.

REFERENCES

1. ERIKSON, ERIK H. "Identity and the Lifecycle," Monograph, *Psychological Issues*, Vol. 1, No. 1, New York: International Universities
   Press, 1959, and ERIKSON, ERIK H., *Childhood and Society*, Second
   Edition, New York: W. W. Norton, 1963.
2. BENEDICT, RUTH, *The Chrysanthemum and the Sword*. Boston: Hough-
   ton Mifflin Company, 1946.
3. EISENBERG, JOHN F. and DILLON, WILTON S., editors. *Man and Beast*:
   Comparative Social Behavior, Washington, D.C.: Smithsonian Insti-
   tution Press, 1971.
4. ROHNER, RONALD R. and KATZ, LEONARD, "Testing for Validity and
   Reliability in Cross-Cultural Research," *American Anthropologist*,
   Vol. 72, No. 5, October, 1970, pp. 1068-1073; and NAROLL, RAOUL,
   "What Have We Learned From Cross-Cultural Surveys?" *American
   Anthropologist*, Vol. 72, No. 6, December, 1970, pp. 1227-1288.

5. TOFFLER, ALVIN, *Future Shock.* New York: Random House, 1970.

6. SAPIR, EDWARD, "Why Cultural Anthropology Needs the Psychiatrist," *Psychiatry,* Vol. 1, No. 1, February, 1938, pp. 7-12; and GALDSTON, IAGO, Ed. *The Interface Between Psychiatry and Anthropology.* New York: Brunner/Mazel Publishers, 1971.

7. MAUSS, MARCEL, *The Gift: Form and Functions of Exchange in Archaic Societies.* Glencoe: The Free Press, 1954 (Translation by Ian Cunnison).

8. CHAPPLE, ELIOT D. and COON, CARLETON S., *Principles of Anthropology,* New York: Henry Holt and Company, 1942; and CHAPPLE, ELIOT D., *Culture and Biological Man.* New York: Holt, Rinehart and Winston, 1970.

9. DILLON, WILTON S., *Gifts and Nations: The Obligation to Give, Receive, and Repay* (with a foreword by Talcott Parsons), The Hague and Paris: Mouton and Ecole Pratique des Hautes Etudes, Sorbonne, 1968. (Distributed in the United States by Humanities Press, New York.)

10. In Larry Ng., ed., *Alternatives to Violence: Stimulus to Dialogue.* New York: Time-Life Books, 1968.

11. BARTON, R. M., *Philippine Pagans.* London, 1938, quoted in Eliot D. Chapple and Carleton S. Coon, *Principles of Anthropology, op. cit.*

12. WRIGHT, QUINCY, "War," in David L. Sills, ed., *International Encyclopedia of Social Sciences.* New York: The Macmillan Company and Free Press, 1968, p. 453.

13. VAYDA, ANDREW P. "Primitive Warfare," in David L. Sills, ed., *International Encyclopedia of the Social Sciences, ibid,* p. 468-472; and VAYDA, ANDREW P., "Hypothesis About Functions of War," in Morton Fried, Marvin Harris, and Robert Murphy, *Wars The Anthropology of Armed Conflict and Aggression.* Garden City: The Natural History Press, 1968, pp. 85-90.

14. CROOK, JOHN H., "Sources of Cooperation in Animals and Man," in John F. Eisenberg and Wilton S. Dillon, *Man and Beast: Comparative Social Behavior, op. cit.,* pp. 235-260.

15. See also MEAD, MARGARET, "Alternatives to War," in Morton Fried, Marvin Harris, and Robert Murphy, editors. *War: The Anthropology of Armed Conflict and Aggression, op. cit.,* pp. 213-228; MEAD, MARGARET, "Violence and Its Regulation," *American Journal of Orthopsychiatry,* Vol. 39, No. 2, March, 1969, pp. 227-229; MEAD, MARGARET, "Bio-Social Components of Political Processes," *Journal of International Affairs,* Vol. 24, No. 1, 1970, pp. 18-28.

16. WHEELER, HARVEY, in Larry Ng, ed., *Alternatives to Violence, op. cit.,* p. 46.

17. ARENDT, HANNAH, *On Violence.* New York: Harcourt, Brace, and World, Inc., 1969, p. 63.

18. DANIELS, DAVID N., GILULA, MARSHALL F., and OCHBERG, FRANK M., editors, *Violence and the Struggle for Existence*. Boston: Little, Brown and Company, 1970.

19. Available through the National Archives, Washington, D.C.

20. BENEDICT, RUTH, *Patterns of Culture*. New York: Houghton Mifflin Company, 1934.

21. CHAGNON, NAPOLEON A., "Yanomamo Social Organization and Warfare," in Symposium on Anthropology and War, American Anthropological Association Plenary Session, 1967. *Natural History* LXXVI, pp. 44-48, 1967.

23. CHAGNON, NAPOLEON A., "The Culture-Ecology of Shifting (Pioneering) Cultivation Among the Yanomamo Indians," *Proceedings VIII International Congress of Anthropological and Ethnological Sciences*, Tokyo, 1968, Vol. 3, pp. 249-255, 1970.

24. CHAGNON, NAPOLEON, A. "The Feast," *Natural History* LXXVI, pp. 34-41, 1968.

25. MALINOWSKI, BRONISLAW, *Argonauts of the Western Pacific*. New York: Dutton & Company, 1953, p. 41.

26. OLIVER, DOUGLAS L., *A Solomon Island Society*. Cambridge: Harvard University Press, 1953.

27. DILLON, WILTON S., "Allah Loves Strong Men," Columbia University Forum, Vol. IV, No. 1 (Winter, 1961), pp. 45-57.

28. TRIANDIS, LEIGH M. and LAMBERT, WILLIAM M., "Sources of Frustration and Targets of Aggression," *Journal of Abnormal and Social Psychology*, Vol. 61, pp. 640-648.

29. DELORIA, VINE, JR., *We Talk, You Listen*. New York: The Macmillan Company, 1970.

30. O'BRIEN, CONOR CRUISE and TOPOLSKI, FELIKS, *The United Nations: Sacred Drama*. New York: Simon and Schuster, 1968.

31. The admission of the People's Republic of China to the United Nations might provide, at least temporarily, some of the elements of the sense of theatre needed to prevent boredom of the world public. The elements of theatre are well described in Francis Fergusson, *The Idea of a Theatre*. Garden City: Doubleday, 1949. Recognizing the United Nations as both a safety valve for releasing tensions and as educational show business would not be inconsistent with the ideas of Richard N. Gardner, "Can the United Nations Be Revised?" *Foreign Affairs*, July, 1970. The importance of such a revival, as a means of controlling the nation-state, is discussed by Frank Tannenbaum, "The Survival of the Fittest," *Columbia University Journal of World Business*, March-April, 1968, pp. 13-20. A valuable "primitive perspective" on the ceremonial and priestly aspects of the United Nations has been provided by David W. Brokensha, "The Leopard-Skin Priest," in Conor Cruise O'Brien and Feliks Topolski, *The United Nations: Sacred Drama, op. cit.*,

pp. 301-308. A good place to start speculating about the importance of humor and laughter, hopefully in high places, is Arthur Koestler, *The Act of Creation.* New York: Macmillan, 1964, and unpublished work of Professor F. L. W. Richardson, University of Virginia. The use of humor to reduce tensions in inter-ethnic relations is described by Melvin Maddocks, "The Age of Touchiness," *Time,* May 10, 1971, p. 21.

32. KOBBEN, ANDRE J. F., "Comparativists and Non-Comparativists in Anthropology," in Raoul Naroll and Ronald Cohen, *A Handbook-Method in Cultural Anthropology,* Garden City: Natural History Press, 1970, pp. 581-596.

5.

Managing Paranoia in Violent Relationships

CHARLES A. PINDERHUGHES, M.D.

PROJECTIVE IDENTIFICATION AND PARANOIA IN
VIOLENT INTERACTIONS

In every case of marital conflict which I have explored, such violence as occurred took place when the party taking violent action perceived the marital partner as an embodiment of evil. One husband perceived the wife as a witch in the moment when his fist was swinging, and the wife, when she later drove her car into his, perceived the husband as a monster. For each person, the same delusion was invariably associated with an act of violence. Each victim was perceived as deserving and needing the act to bring it to justice, to correct some defect, to produce better behavior, or to make it more thoughtful and responsive.

In every case, the perpetrator of violence in marital conflict was experiencing intense emotion associated with a false belief-system that was based upon a renounced part of the self. An hysterical wife had renounced control and discipline in her search for freedom of spirit and expression. She experienced her obsessional husband's disciplined and structured life as an attempt to stifle her and deprive her of life. The obsessional husband had renounced and warded off emotions and spontaneity. He perceived the hysterical wife as primitive, sick, uncontrolled, irresponsible, manipulating and evil.

Each perceived the other as an enemy who was threatening existence. Careful study has revealed that in these instances the enemy always represented a renounced and projected part of the self, which, in the moment of violence, was perceived as totally evil. In the moment of violence, love for and identification with the object were renounced. In nonviolent moments the marital partners had a more balanced view of each other, and they even idealized each other at times. Clearly they lived in a complementary relationship, with each needing the other to restore the renounced lost part of himself.

Every destructive act is aimed at someone or something which is viewed as deserving the act. The devaluation of victims is found in the case of acts less passionate than those described, and even in the case of calculated acts of violence. A person who has been assaulted and robbed has commonly been considered stupid to have been in the circumstances which made victimization possible, or even to have invited and deserved what happened by being present and available. Devaluation and blaming of the victims serve the witnesses of violence as well as the perpetrators by reducing the pain which would otherwise be experienced through identification, sparing them the guilt and the need for reaction, while giving indignation a target that is weak, wounded, and unlikely to strike back.

It is not possible to do violence without projecting evil onto the person, group, or other object of violence. (Even the surgeon must conceptualize the infection, tumor or other operative target as evil in order to make his incision.) This does not mean that there is no reality to the complaint. It does mean the maintenance of an unbalanced, idealized view of oneself and one's position and an unbalanced, denigrated view of the object and its position. It means also that some content is projected from within the self and perceived as external; this content may correspond to some of the external facts. Violence to another cannot occur in a moment of introjective relationship, when the would-be victim is perceived as an acknowledged and valued part of the self. Violence can only occur under circumstances of projective relationship. Paranoid dynamics with false belief systems based on projection can be observed in the midst of all intended violent human interactions. Moreover, paranoid dynamics and content may be present for varying periods of time before and after the violence.

Human beings all over the earth have processed and programmed into their individual and group life dual paranoid processes which glorify selves and vilify outsiders, or vice versa (1). The processing is successful in that we do not perceive and acknowledge our own false beliefs and violence, but we clearly perceive the false beliefs and violence of others.

The use of projective mechanisms, of false belief systems, and of frank paranoid behavior is far commoner than we acknowledge. In fact, it occurs in every individual, and it may dominate the behavior of many healthy persons. We acknowledge the existence of paranoia only in persons whose capacity to trust and to relate introjectively with affectionate bonds to other human beings is so impaired that they are unable to align their paranoid processes and content with those of relatives, friends, schoolmates, or culture-mates. We paranoids who have the capacity to trust and to relate introjectively with affectionate bonds to other human beings align our paranoid processes with those of our fellow group members, becoming Catholics, Protestants or Jews, Democrats, Socialists or Republicans, Russians, Vietnamese or Norwegians, Africans, Europeans or Americans, behaviorists, psychoanalysts or existentialists, and so forth.

The content of our paranoia identifies us, and cements us into groups. However, we carefully avoid recognition of this paranoia by labeling it as a religion, an ideological position, a school of thought, or an ethnocentric perception. It is non-pathological since our capacity for trusting and for forming introjective relations with many other human beings is unimpaired.

As long as we use the capacity for introjective identification with some persons and employ projective identifications with other persons, we shall have uncontrolled group-related paranoia and violence in human inter-group behavior.

PSYCHOPHYSIOLOGICAL PATTERNS ASSOCIATED WITH VIOLENCE

Dichotomy and antagonism are present in the organization of human behavior at every level. The dichotomous and antagonistic patterns in vegetative physiological processes program conflict and ambivalence into psychological processes (2). Primitive paranoid patterns, by aggrandizing one side and denigrating the other, separate the paired components of conflicting psychological situations, permitting one component to be accepted and the other to be rejected. This paranoid resolution, leading to introjective relationships with affectionate bonds to one object and to projective relationships with aggressive bonds to another, provides the basic capacities for peace and harmony as well as for conflict and violence. It is an ubiquitous process. Resolution of the oedipal conflict is achieved in this manner, as the establishment of an affectionate bond with the parental object of introjective relationship and of an aggressive bond with the parental object of projective relationship develops. Less ambivalent relationships are thus achieved, as one parent becomes more regularly the object of affection and the other more regularly the object of aggression.

Aggression, conflict, and violence, which were previously distributed between both parents, become reinforced toward one and inhibited toward the other. Conflict and violence may more easily take place in interactions with objects of a projective relationship and uniting, conjugating, and protective alliances and group formation can more easily take place with objects of introjective relationship.

When a group is formed, the paranoid patterns in an individual are reinforced and aligned with similar patterns in others.

During resolution of the oedipal conflict, the ambivalence of early childhood is resolved by the development of a predominantly introjective relationship with one parent and projective relationship with the other parent. Physiological mechanisms mediating approach behavior become associated more closely with one parent while physiological mechanisms mediating avoidance behavior become more associated with the other parent. Physiological mechanisms which mediate avoidance behavior also mediate projective and aggressive behavior. In most cultures they are reinforced in males. Physiological mechanisms which mediate approach behavior also mediate introjective and nurturing behavior and in most cultures are reinforced in females. The objects which become associated with physiological patterns mediating projective and aggressive behavior are more likely to be objects of violence. Linkages between certain objects and physiological patterns mediating aggression occur in the first year of life. So-called "stranger anxiety" reflects the association of avoidance patterns with unfamiliar persons. During the same period, approach patterns become associated with familiar persons. Thus, from a very early age psychophysiological patterns mediating seeking behavior become associated with "one's own" and psychophysiological patterns mediating avoidance behavior become associated with outsiders, and paranoid mechanisms aggrandizing one's own and denigrating outsiders begin to develop. An attack from one's own engenders a sense of pain, loss, and inner hurt, while attack from an outsider engenders a sense of threat or anger and violent responses. To eliminate the pain of attack from one's own, we must rid ourselves of the introjected object and control or destroy it in an ejecting and projecting process. The marital partners cited at the beginning of this paper related to one another by introjective and projective processes alternately. One question which we address today is: how is it possible for such persons to develop alternatives?

AN ALTERNATIVE TO VIOLENCE IN MARITAL INTERACTION

During a year of individual psychotherapy and six months of conjoint therapy, the marital partners cited greatly improved their ability to limit destructive behavior and to manage rage. However, rage reactions with paranoid views and fantasies of violence continued until the paranoid mechanisms of both partners were demonstrated to them in conjoint sessions. When I had successfully demonstrated their paranoia to them, each partner began to interpret the statements of the other as projections, initially using the interpretations as verbal brickbats in their encounters. Each attack, when shown to be based upon projection, was followed by sheepishness and guilt in the attacker. The paranoia of each was rapidly undermined as each increasingly realized that every statement made about another person is true of oneself. Banter and laughter had replaced hostile encounters by the fourth interview of this kind. Care had been taken not to favor one over the other, and verbatim notes were recorded and used to demonstrate the projection used in each accusation.

Paranoid and aggressive behavior is often employed by one party to control, manipulate or exploit another. When we can successfully demonstrate that all the content one imputes to another is a projection from oneself, the paranoia may be recognized and the aggression controlled. I have used this method successfully with two couples, with two families, and with several individual patients where violent behavior was among the presenting complaints. Periodic reinforcements of the favorable results may be needed. The existence of a positive transference and a therapeutic alliance, and the acknowledgment of paranoid thinking and behavior by all people, including the therapist, were important factors in reducing resistance to the interpretations.

When we become able to reduce our narcissistic and self-aggrandizing characteristics enough to perceive our behavior objectively, we shall see that paranoid mechanisms pervade all normal thinking and behavior. The paranoias associated with introjective mechanisms aggrandize objects and are associated with delusions of love, while the paranoias associated with projective mechanisms denigrate objects and are associated with unfavorable social discrimination and often with violence.

The acknowledgment by all psychiatrists of their own non-pathological paranoias and their own violent impulses and behavior could provide an important and useful model for other individuals, groups, and institutions who also identify the paranoia and violence of others while they are singularly unable to perceive and acknowledge their own.

PARANOIA IN ORGANIZED VIOLENCE-PRONE SOCIETIES

In every organized society there are aggrandized, more powerful and privileged élites and devalued, less powerful, less privileged, and often dehumanized non-élites. Élites and non-élites are determined by power struggles for dominant roles, for resources, and for special privilege.

Periodic violence is common in the interactions between élite and non-élite groups. Even more common are the extensive, slow, attenuated, destructive effects which élites bring about in non-élites without recognizing what they are doing.

Élites promote among themselves and among non-élites beliefs in their special-ness and superiority based upon their conspicuous possession or acquisition of selected attributes, or resources. Social structures are developed to ensure that the élites retain guardianship over the selected attributes or resources and to guarantee that non-élites have only limited access to them. In the relationships between the two groups, élites are primarily paranoid and narcissistic and relate to non-élites by projection. Non-élites are primarily dependent but share the false belief system of the élites by identification with the aggressor. Thus the non-élites project on and dump on themselves, compounding their dependency with depression and varying degrees of disorganization, and thereby "validating" and further reinforcing the paranoia and narcissism of the élites.

In the life of each person the often violent struggle for services, resources, and the privilege of having others respond to one's demands begins at birth. Initially the infant is the élite, the master; the parent is the slave. The infant initiates demands and exercises power without respect for the parent's problems, and, if the relationship is to continue, the parent accedes and accommodates, sometimes willingly, sometimes not.

As growth processes make voluntary behavior and accommodation by the child possible, parents initiate demands and exercise power, and, if the relationship is to continue, the child accedes and accommodates, sometimes willingly, sometimes not. Parents become the élite, the master; children, the slaves. A period of latency intervenes in this struggle, since each individual child ordinarily is no match for the coalition of organized and institutionalized parental power outside and the internalized parental power of his superego.

At puberty, growth processes provide physical, mental, and emotional reinforcements to the child, who revives the struggle for freedom from enslaving external and internal forces. By solitary struggle, the child-youth cannot ordinarily gain freedom from enslaving external and internal forces, and compliant behavior or neurotic products of repression emerge. Moreover, the freedom achieved through solitary struggle often leaves isolated or psychotic persons with unmet needs for satisfying attachments. It is by organizing and forming alliances that youths achieve most success in their struggle toward freedom. Unwittingly they become enslaved to the new alliances and groups of which they find themselves a part, and all the earlier dynamic struggles continue under new names and with a new cast of characters. The struggles continue in friendships, marriages, clubs, organizations, classes, castes and races; we seek social arrangements which will reduce the struggles and produce more mutuality. Regardless of the process or structure produced, our behavior within it remains the same. An élite, more powerful initiating party and a relatively deprived, less powerful accommodat-

ing party emerge in a dynamic interaction which may appear
to have states of relative equilibrium.

We have not underestimated the more visible power
processes in these dynamic interactions between élites and
non-élites. The black psychoanalyst, Franz Fanon, dramati-
cally described them in this century, and the white Juan
Luis Vives described them in the 16th century (3, 4). Common, ordinary people have been describing these processes
since human societies began, but without acknowledgment,
since only the élite (the leader, the head) can have intelli-
gence, be an initiator, or make pronouncements to which
others should listen.

Élites are influential people who employ direct and processed violence to alter social structure and other realities
into alignment with their beliefs. The falseness of their beliefs is not evident, since reality is contrived to express the
beliefs and make them appear true. While the resources and
power of élites are clearly evident, their paranoia is apt to
be well camouflaged.

Élite individuals, or people feeling at home in an élite
country, consider themselves to be well developed, resource-
ful, independent, advanced, and mature in relation to non-
élites who are perceived as underdeveloped, dependent, less
mature, and more primitive. Every unit of social organization has its élites and non-élites, and even within a single
individual, there are élite and non-élite aspects. Within the
context of each social organization, both élites and non-élites
share the delusions of the élites and are quite unaware that
the beliefs are false, since contrived realities are forcibly maintained to provide the impression that the beliefs are true.

Only in an era when influential élites experience a rising
sense of guilt and shame about the plight of non-élites can
élites develop reform movements. Reform movements reduce
the disparity between élites and non-élites in resources,

power, and privilege. They reduce the guilt and shame of the élites and mitigate the suffering of non-élites. Reform may reinforce the shared paranoia as the gratitude of non-élites and the sense of "noblesse oblige" in élites encourage both groups to endorse their disparate roles and the false beliefs associated with them.

If they feel that élites show consideration and generosity, non-élites may accept the disparate roles and the value and belief systems which aggrandize élites. They are unaware that they are being rewarded, paid, and bribed to believe.

Men and women, employers and employees, whites and blacks, parents and children, educators and students, rich and poor, colonial powers and the colonized, and other complementary paired groups have functioned in our society with disparate relationships and associated false belief systems maintained by bribery as often as by force.

Traditionally, initiating has been the responsibility of élites and masters; accommodating has been the responsibility of non-élites and slaves. Intense conflict and violence are apt to occur when non-élites become initiators.

THE USE OF CONFRONTATION IN THE MANAGEMENT OF GROUP-RELATED PARANOIA

Until the 1960's white Americans were able to have it both ways—to be devout racists and true believers in democracy. Whites in the South were scapegoated as the racist ones, while the whites in the rest of the country, feeling purified by projecting their racism upon Southerners, maintained the delusion that they were democratic. In the confrontations of the 1960's, as racism throughout the country became more visible, whites outside the South took back their projections upon Southerners. Unfortunately, the projections of whites upon blacks are not so easy to reverse, for the persistent, contrived cultural pressures from two centuries of the most coercive and destructive slave system our world has known have produced in the experience of black people qualities which invite projection and reinforce false beliefs about blacks. In fact, it was not until 1966 that large numbers of black people became aware that they shared the pro-white anti-black paranoia of other Americans. Therapeutic efforts to undo this among blacks gave rise to the Black Power Movement.

In 1968 I noted (5) that: "The Black Power class of reactions involves disparity in paired parties, with one in power and the other in dependency, when the dependent party seeks peer status while the party in power resists. Conflicts between labor and management, women suffragettes and men, college students and college administrators, and between adolescents and adults are well-known examples of this class of reactions.

"The fact that they are often managed badly with unnecessary conflict, and at times riots, reflects primarily the unrecognized immature motivations of persons in power, whose lack of understanding, use of power, sense of entitlement, and lack of cooperation are retained from early childhood patterns. They denigrate others and aggrandize themselves. They use their intellects in the service of the pleasure principle primarily to supply reasons and methods of continuing and enlarging present comforts for those with whom they identify regardless of the price paid by others. They are more responsive to the needs of a single individual with whom they identify than to a million individuals they see as outsiders. Not only are they unconscious of the infantile nature of their behavior but they unwittingly employ their resources to create an illusion of maturity in themselves.

"People with power to influence social structure frequently are unconscious victims of pathogenic projections derived from the body image, which have been reinforced by the groups to which they belong. These basic psychological processes which generate false beliefs are shared by all people."

When a more powerful party dominates a less powerful and more dependent one, the dependent party is brainwashed toward participation in shared false beliefs, a *folie à deux*, in which both parties aggrandize the more powerful and denigrate the less powerful party.

When such a paranoid belief-system has been projected into the structuring of grossly unequal complementary roles, characteristic dynamics occur when the weaker party attempts to undo the beliefs and equalize the roles through confrontation processes. The narcissism and delusions of the more powerful party may be thrown into bold relief as they militantly resist or attempt to repress, disperse, or discredit the weaker party. Concerning these dynamics I also noted in 1968 (5) that: "Primitive patterns, reinforced by groups, determine the thinking and feeling of group members toward one another and toward outsiders. To change primitive thinking patterns, primitive methods are needed.

"When thinking patterns are unresponsive to reason, pleasure or pain—in the form of reward or power—is required to change them. Where rewards are not forthcoming, power is required to produce the necessary emotional crisis. When the crisis is over, the rate of change declines sharply. A social order unresponsive to reason requires repeated crises for significant change.

"In the absence of an effective agency of conscience within government, popular dissent must be the principal source of the creative conflict which is necessary for important changes in a stable social system. This leaves government in the role of adversary to those who seek constructive change in government. A federal department of values, ethics, and national conscience and its counterpart in local governments and in other institutions would ensure more healthy creative conflict within government as well as between government and dissenting citizens.

"The treatment of pathogenic racial conflict and the crippling pathology associated with it ideally should be the treatment of the paranoiac, phobic, and anxiety patterns underlying white racism. This will require undoing of the projections of whites on blacks. Since blacks have been so altered as to make the projections seem realistic, only alterations in blacks can offer whites an opportunity to perceive blacks in a different light and thereby modify the racism of which they are unconscious.

"The Black Power movement produces, at one and the same time, the crisis needed to make change possible and different mental representations out of which whites and blacks can build a new image of blacks. During the crisis period, when there is a great uncertainty about what will develop, primitive psychological patterns will be activated in more and more whites. Accompanying the Black Power movement are rising conflict and anxiety in whites and increasing confidence and self-esteem among blacks, who perceive the importance and rightness of the Black Power movement in the eradication of racism."

One white person described his concern about confrontations in the following way: "My home community in New York is frightening and explosive now. They used to ignore one another. Now there is a personal encounter every time two persons brush against one another. I now fear for my father. His angry outbursts used to be ignored, but now they lead to confrontations wherever he goes and whenever he behaves as he always has. He never had any sensitivity to the reactions of others, so that he doesn't know when he is getting into serious conflict. His station in life [business owner in black community] used to protect him, but no longer. He always had very little control of his temper and felt somebody was doing something to him. I used to identify with his victims when he verbally attacked them, but now people are so responsive, I fear for him."

In this age of dissent, black people, poor people, the underrewarded and unrespected, the college students, and youth throughout the land have bombarded and loosened the forces that have disciplined our society, however inequitably. Increases in crime, immorality, and riots reflect both the relaxed discipline and the disillusionment with existing values, policies, and practices. "We have been brought to a point of national identity crisis. Will our national character undergo the maturation toward democracy of which it is capable if enough influential persons insist upon change? Or will the same primitive paranoid forces remain in the driver's seat, buttressed and augmented by invocation and organization of greater power?" In 1968 I closed a presentation with the above questions, which have been only partially answered. Some trends in both directions have taken place.

During the 1960's a series of major confrontations has occurred. The confrontations of the integration movement revealed disparities between our beliefs and our behavior and were uniting in direction. The militant White Power movement of 1965, called the "White Backlash," undermined integration efforts and was divisive and polarizing in direction. Blacks responded with the counter-militant Black Power movement. The new group feeling and militant spirit escalated confrontations between blacks and whites. Whites altered structure and increased integration at the black-white interface while increasing repression elsewhere. Confrontations spread to all areas of social discrimination. A series of assassinations and a remarkably senseless war confronted us further with our violence and inhumanity.

If human beings were reasonable creatures, confrontations would not be so essential to the process of introducing new ideas and new possibilities of thinking. Instead of being reasonable, human beings employ their reason as a tool in the service of people and beliefs with which they identify and to gratify self-interest of various kinds. Reason employed in the service of narcissistic or paranoid interests regularly results in exploitation and damage to others. We have developed ability to recognize narcissism and paranoia in individuals, but when many individuals align their narcissism and paranoia with one another, so that they share beliefs and bonds of affection and trust along with the experience of distrust and aggression toward outsiders, we are curiously unaccustomed to defining or recognizing such behavior as unreasonable.

Reason is also employed to legitimize and process such force and violence as are needed to structure the world to fit our false beliefs. By forming groups and using various forms of demonstrations, protests, and demands, compartmentalized social structure may be loosened, as engagement, communication, and encounters over issues occur. The spectrum of confrontation goes from passive protest at one pole to violent revolution at the other.

As the enforced projections embedded in a social system are undermined, flexibility develops in social structure and roles. Upper-class folk come to more freely enjoy lower-body, lower-class things and lower-class folk participate more in upper-body, upper-class activities.

A few years ago one of my patients spontaneously remarked in an interview, "I really don't believe we think of the Vietnamese as people. As soon as we do—we will be unable to kill them as we are doing. We could only drop an atom bomb on Orientals. We could never have done that to white people. Somehow we always forget the dignity of the other person and somehow we are always considering the dignity of a few that we associate with. An Armenian man recently said to a Jewish friend of mine, 'I'm glad you are going to help your people.' " The patient went on to say, "I am not Jewish but I am white, and I, too, want to get involved—to be active, to get out and slug and to get on top. It certainly is a shame how we get caught up in our day-to-day difficulties and forget the beauty. I saw a gentle movie that brought tears to my eyes. I am awed by the perfection of the situation with babies. That nursing situation—with one needing the other. It is so perfect for both of them—but in the actual child-rearing, it isn't possible to see the beauty. As Carlos was developing, I took pride in his gains and his beauty—but—DAMN IT! I must be handling him too permissively. He started asserting himself and would say, 'I stay here' or 'I want to do it myself,' To get him to go with me, I'd end up hitting him and he'd scream the whole way. I'd stoop to subterfuge—candy and other bribery. That's terrible—but it's better than slugging him—and it eases the way. DAMN IT! He's my oppressor! He limits me and hampers me and he keeps deciding not to go along with whatever the family is doing. Sometimes I feel he is not human at all but just a little monster. He is always confronting me with the fact that he's a different individual—with his own ideas that should be respected. If he weren't my own child—I'd kill him!—but in this confrontation—I have to swallow my pride and see how selfish and violent I am. Reluctantly I modify my position to take his needs into account. I even go further. I know it is important to save face for him so that I am trying to develop ways to have my way with him without him feeling it is imposed."

This example reflects a problem which is often encountered when there is great disparity in the resources and power between two parties, when the more powerful party accepts without question an élitist value system and belief system which justifies and rationalizes the unequal relationship. With a complete sense of righteousness and often with good will, the party in power perceives the behavior of the dissenters as unwise, unreasonable and destructive.

Any belief-system which we hold is associated with physiological patterns that are linked to vital processes in our bodies. Confrontations produce a sense of threat of body change. It is for this reason that the challenging of any long-standing belief causes an aggressive response in those who hold the belief.

Each college president may plan to keep his "cool" and to affectionately welcome all students who seek his assistance, but when the campus activists invade his office with their non-negotiable demands, he responds with aggression and rage and is unable to see that his own behavior is being mirrored by the students. He is unable to perceive that he does not own his office any more than they. Until the confrontation he is unable to perceive how helpless and small he is and the extent to which the constituents whom he seeks to rule have granted him all that he has.

Authority stimulates fantasies associated with power, control, and narcissism. These fantasies ride "piggy-back" on all the thoughts of realistically-oriented behavior. The president's good deeds bear witness to his service and humanitarian motivations but, at the same time, hide his narcissism and paranoia until the confrontation occurs.

We have underestimated the physiological nature of such reactions. Whatever space or activity becomes identified with one's person through linkages in the body image, becomes firmly entrenched unconscious perception in one's own possession. Under this circumstance, rage is natural and predictable, as one's person is invaded or parts of one's body taken over by another. Andrenergic physiology, once stimulated in our hypothetical college president, will require that he think and behave defensively and aggressively.

The extent to which we get unconscious gratification from roles we have and from props around us varies greatly. Each parent wants his children to grow and to become mature but resists their struggles for independence when his parental role is threatened. The teacher wants the student to learn, but not to learn so much that the teacher's role is threatened. In these confrontations, encounters, and dynamic struggles, everyone has the opportunity and experiences pressure toward change, and, as a rule, is changed. Everyone develops as complementary unequal relationships, such as the parent-child and teacher-pupil relationships, can move toward a peer status in which there are more inter-dependence and sharing in the general relationships. Thus, confrontation processes may be the basic essential process of education and of growth in beliefs and behavior, which are to take place wherever unequal human relationships have existed.

An analogous disparity in power may exist between aspects of a single personality, with one part of the personality dominating, enslaving, or exploiting another. Confrontation often reveals internal conflicts in the personalities of both the confronter and those confronted, which, prior to the confrontation, were camouflaged and invisible. Perhaps psychiatrists should give more attention to the potential for achieving internal psychological confrontations with subsequent modifications in the relationships between various aspects of the personality.

It is quite possible that this method of initiating psychological and behavioral change may be far more effective than verbal methods of other less conflict-filled methods. Confrontation methods and psychotherapy methods have many elements in common in their goals, methods, and results. Both press toward changes in psychology and behavior.

However, psychotherapy approaches tend to emphasize alliances and more disciplined, and even obsessional, management of conflict. Confrontation processes emphasize the importance of conflict and crises as circumstances necessary for the achievement of change. Each process can be used to augment the other. Personally, I have employed confrontation tactics with therapeutic effect in patients who resist change, and I have found the use of interpretation and development of positive alliances to be an extremely useful addition in conducting confrontation processes toward conclusions which are gratifying to all parties in the engagement. When well conducted, such engagement not infrequently results in a new more satisfying and more equitable marriage.

Listed below are some aspects of group dynamics which are relatable to confrontation processes.

1. Confrontations will occur as long as there is unequal value assigned to talking and listening, putting out and taking in.
2. A confrontation process offers the only way to deal with an omnipotent or stubborn (or phallic) opposition in a relatively short time.
3. With confrontation, there is a high value placed upon the verbal, emotional, and physical interactions of persons who are ordinarily barred from them by existing social structure.
4. Reinforcement of introjective-incorporative patterns in leaders reduces the need for confrontation. Increase in the glorification of leaders, or of phallic, aggressive, competitive, and other victim-creating behavior, reinforces the need for confrontation, if change is to occur. Confrontation is less necessary for persons who are introspective and self-inquiring. Those who perceive violent motivations in themselves are less apt to impute by projection violent motivations to others.

5. Each individual and each institution should be pressured to live up to its avowed code. Practices should be consistent with principles, and behavior consistent with codes, laws, and ethics. Each institution should relate to its code at the same time it is relating to outsiders.

6. Confrontation often reveals immature aspects of persons in authority.

7. Confrontation disrupts artificial, contrived social structure, which separates people and supports false beliefs about them. With the contrived social structures we have, it is hard to believe in the equal, human worth of the president of the corporation and the laborer who is digging ditches for the corporation.

   Once divested of the props of the office, of the disciplined structure maintained by power and force, presidents and laborers can experience encounters in which their equality can be perceived. The legend and fiction about princes or kings who disguise themselves as beggars to walk among their people reflect a general awareness of this. One trustee of a university talked with me about being trapped and held captive for several hours with a large body of students who did not know his identity. He was able to identify with the students enough to function as a unifying force in subsequent encounters between students and trustees.

8. Confrontation is a symptomatic treatment which deals with the paranoia, but it does not prevent élitist-oriented paranoia from being built into the new system which is created. Somehow human beings always contrive new systems which have élitist aspects.

9. Freedom can never come until we think in terms of freedom from paranoia.

10. There is a systematic reinforcement of projective

mechanisms in the thinking and behavior of soldiers, policemen, and others who deal with authorized violence. We also reinforce negative projections upon the victims of socially authorized violence.

11. The need for confrontation may be increased when enveloping, restricting, confining, incorporating, restraining, imprisoning behavior is dominant. These behaviors are not generally perceived as violent until the physical structure of the object is altered, as by crushing or bruising. Violence is defined more in terms of tissue damage or in terms of phallic, intrusive behavior.

Concepts of violence are reserved for behavior associated with masculine fantasies. Yet enveloping, imprisoning behavior may be an equally victimizing stimulus to confrontation, although it is associated with feminine fantasies. Sudden, direct violence is generally associated with masculine fantasies, while slow processed violence is usually associated with feminine fantasies.

12. In authoritative groups, scapegoating occurs downward, while in truly democratic groups scapegoating occurs upward as well as downward. In a group-oriented democracy, the leader is not glorified, and the group members may develop considerable power and authority. The leader is as eligible for scapegoating as other group members and may be scapegoated more than the other members whenever there is much dissatisfaction. When groups are leader-centered and led by authoritarian leaders, the leaders are glorified and the group members have little power and authority. The leader is less eligible for scapegoating than group members, and when dissatisfaction occurs, group members tend to be scapegoated instead of the leader. Repeated victimization of scapegoats by the leaders may stimulate group members to develop the power and

group identity required to confront, control or neutralize the downward scapegoating process.

13. Confrontation permits identification of the violent ones in new directions. Potential for violence and use of violence is often projected upon "low," controlled people. Confrontations quite regularly reveal that the users of force and violence are the "high," controlling people. However, we seldom define official behavior as violent, as long as the victims are generally accepted targets of aggression and denigrating false beliefs. Confrontation thus permits the development of new and more realistic definitions. Confrontations concerning social inequities or the Vietnam War bring into more minds doubts about definitions and old patterns of behavior and consideration of new definitions and new patterns of behavior which are more harmonious with our values. Televised movies of war as it really is—of wounds, of screaming, of death as they are actually happening—would provide a confrontation for citizens and officials in every country which could less easily be denied and rationalized away.

14. Confrontation is an educational process with learning aspects; confrontation is a therapeutic process which corrects paranoia in individuals; confrontation is a reform process which can correct social problems; confrontation has sociological features since it can lead to new alignments between persons in different groups.

15. Confrontation deals with the interaction of persons with separate and different positions and there lies beyond this stage of relationship a stage of placing high value upon the fusion, complementarity, and synchrony of the behavior of all parties. This stage, in turn, prepares the way for a humanized orchestration of highly valued roles in a more inclusive, more harmonious society.

In every society, in every relationship, and in every personality there are self-oriented narcissistic components which seek an élite initiating role with sufficient power and resources to ensure that other components will accommodate to the sense of entitlement and special privilege assumed by the élites. Élites further ensure that non-élites will be controlled while élites are more free. Élites are more protected and less accessible. Non-élites have very little access to the special characteristics arbitrarily used to define the élite (money, education, resources, etc.).

Élites invariably maintain paranoid belief systems which aggrandize themselves and denigrate non-élites. Non-élites share these beliefs, denigrate themselves and, for this reason, are inclined toward depression and disorganization or organized in a manner which subordinates their interests to those of the élites. This is the basic nature of social oppression wherever it is found.

When the oppressed seek freedom from self-denigrating beliefs, they no longer glorify élites and confrontations occur.

When the deprived seek a greater share of limited resources, confrontations occur.

When previously accommodating parties try to initiate, confrontations occur.

Confrontations occur because most persons are intimately attached to the beliefs, roles, and resources which they identify with themselves and are unable to identify with outsiders. Because of linkages in the body image, sharing a role or resource and changing a belief are perceived as losses of important parts of one's self.

Primitive psychophysiological paranoid processes dominate our behavior when we organize in groups, and until we learn more about them, they can be contained and managed only by confrontation processes.

Non-pathological, group-related paranoid processes involving élites and non-élites are found all over the earth. They are often associated with violence and are especially resistant to change.

The concepts presented suggest that non-pathological paranoid processes are rooted in biological patterns and cannot be eradicated, but may be better controlled by giving attention to the following guidelines:

a) Reinforce incorporating, affiliative processes.

b) Recognize that because mental representations of body, of clothing, and of social structure are interrelated in the body image, loosening of bodies, of clothing, and of values related to these must accompany loosening of social structure.

c) Define violence and social discrimination according to the perception of the victim. Violence should be defined in terms of perceptual experience as well as in terms of motor acts.

d) Have each individual and each group conduct self inquiries about prejudice and violence. Recognize and acknowledge our helplessness, inadequacy, frailty and dependency instead of denying them in ourselves and imputing them to others.

e) Develop sensitivity to and awareness of the projected false components in behavior.

f) Establish superordinate goals for conflicting persons and groups. Glorify behavior which produces genuine peace, harmony, unity, and justice.

g) Remember that dominant parties generally relate by projection while subordinate parties relate by identification and introjection of the aggressor.

h) Manage adversary relationships by employing processes which advance the identification of hostile parties with one another.

i) Constructively manage confrontation and encounter processes by helping the more powerful parties to become aware of their paranoia and to perceive in the confrontation an opportunity to improve relationships collaboratively.

j) Carefully evaluate the meaning of any overvaluation or denigration, of division into "good" and "bad" or "high" and "low," of a sense of special-ness or entitlement, which are expressed by you or those around you.

k) Avoid segmental approaches to reality. Use holistic approaches which examine all parties and weigh the interests of self and others equally. Give parallel attention to inner and outer aspects of self and of each person encountered. Develop alliances between different levels and different compartments of social structures.

l) Remember that when we encounter content which "blows our mind," one of our basic beliefs has been challenged. Avoid paranoid and defensive responses, work through resistances to the suggestion and consider it seriously.

m) Social discrimination embedded in an institution may be reduced by altering the organization and relationships so that: (1) there is sharing of power; (2) there are no closed dominant-subordinate relationships (i.e., no uni-directional hierarchical relationships); (3) there are no exclusive groups; (4) feedback mechanisms communicate the responses engendered by all official actions; (5) there is no aggrandizement and no denigration; (6) there are no human targets of hostile aggression; (7) there is reduction of emotionalism and intensity of interaction; (8) there is integration of élite and non-élite persons; (9) rising of the lower and underdeveloped people is facilitated; (10) speech and clothing are not restricted so long as they are not harmful; and (11) two-way ratings and two-way supervision between supervisors and supervisees are employed.

n) Learn to distrust what you see and hear.

We have come to trust what we see and hear, forgetting that in the moment when we respond to a stimulus, there occurs an instantaneous fusion of that stimulus with the rapid succession of (physiological) responses within us, which are then imputed by projection to the outside world. We do not adequately recognize that perception itself is basically a non-pathological paranoid process based on projection. Moreover, vision and hearing permit perception, classification, interpretation and judgment to be made about an object before it is close enough to be harmful. This reinforced the usefulness and value of projective and paranoid mechanisms early in man's history when harm or violence were likely to come from outside sources. In the present, men's projections and paranoid beliefs themselves have become the principal source of violence to humans.

Since the end of World War II almost eight million human beings have been killed by other human beings in tribal-type warfare and many times more have been injured in violent interactions (6).

o) Remember that reason more often leads one astray than to the truth. Research has often been misused to determine the extent to which some facts may be found which conform to and support false beliefs. Most studies are constructed primarily to support one's own beliefs or to do violence to someone else's.

In most instances, what is perceived as violent and destructive stimulates violent response. The quiet violence produced by discrimination in social arrangements has stimulated both revolution and reform. Excluded and deprived individuals and groups have learned the power of non-negotiable demands and confrontation. In the vigorous encounters which follow, paranoia and processed violence are thrown into bold relief. Under those circumstances élites and non-élites commonly find themselves engaged in conflict-laden integrative activity in which cherished behavior, values, beliefs, and standards are altered.

Gains originally made by élites at the expense of broader humanitarian goals are reversed, and élites experience losses and feel violated by any broad humaitarian reforms which follow.

While overt physical violence may not occur, the non-pathological group-related paranoia is just as rampant and just as difficult to manage. Violent behavior is commonly an expression of paranoia or of a counter-paranoid attempt to control it. The development of power and use of confrontation and encounter process are often unsuitable, since this course may further polarize the parties, reinforcing their paranoia and potential for violence.

Massive programs of research on the non-pathological paranoia in all sectors of society are indicated, but they are unlikely to come about, since paranoids are unaware that their beliefs are false and are too narcissistic to look for negative attributes in themselves. Short of such programs, we can only stumble toward improved understanding and hope to get enough to warrant the public health and education programs which may, to some other generation, offer alternatives.

REFERENCES

1. PINDERHUGHES, C. A., "The Universal Resolution of Ambivalence by Paranoia with an Example in Black and White." *Amer. J. Psychother.* 24:597-610, 1970.

2. PINDERHUGHES, C. A., "Somatic, Psychic, and Social Sequellae of Loss."
Presented at joint meeting of American Psychoanalytic and American Psychiatric Associations, Miami Beach, Florida, May 5, 1969.

3. FANON, F., *The Wretched of the Earth.* New York: Grove Press, 1963.

4. ZILBOORG, G., *A History of Medical Psychology.* New York: W. W. Norton and Company, 1941, pp. 180-195.

5. PINDERHUGHES, C. A., "Understanding Black Power: Processes and Proposals." *Amer. J. Psychiat.* 125:1552-1557, May 1969.

6. Bulletin of the Research Institute of America, Inc. 589 5th Ave., New York. Vol. 19, No. 23, June 7, 1968.

6.

Discussion

1. HOWARD P. ROME, M.D.
2. LOUIS JOLYON WEST, M.D.

1. HOWARD P. ROME, M.D.

O F LATE I HAVE BEEN intrigued by rereading the activities of
the late Ignatius Donnelly, a fellow Minnesotan who was
prominent in the Mid-West version of the populist movement
in the early part of this century. To say the least, Donnelly
was a stormy petrel who epitomized in his life, writings, and
the fizzled social revolution he tried to promote among his
fellow Mid-Western agrarians the paradox our speakers have
referred to: the social change that only now, years later, is
being seen in elevated profile.

It is a challenge of the first order of magnitude to dis-
cuss these eloquent, comprehensive and provocative papers.

We, who are gathered in Washington, will be witness to
yet another ritualized demonstration this coming week. We
will have a front seat to a live-action demonstration of what
some feel are the alternatives to violence as the local law
enforcement authority implements them. We all hope they

will be made the wiser by a full and complete understanding of past events of a similar nature.

A commonly held premise holds that man should act as a rational creature committed to logical behavior. The history of recent and past events asserts that this is manifestly naive. Man is reasonable and acts logically only erratically when it serves his interests. We psychiatrists can attest to the truth of this from long, painful, and personal experience with our particular contact with those victims of evil of yet another brand. The Appellate Court of the District of Columbia recently has addressed itself to that brand of violence. As Pogo wryly observed: "We have met the enemy and he is us."

Professor Sanford vividly made this point in his reference to acting-out the aggressive fantasies of the masses. It also was the rationalization that produced the almost unbelievable explanation about the destruction of Bon Tre. The Army's briefing officer, as you may recall, with astounding aplomb said: "We had to destroy the village to save it!"

Doctor Dillon gave us the aphorism that symbolizes these incredible and parlous times when he characterized the recent exchange of reciprocity responses as: Ying cum Yang; Ping cum Pong. His motion picture of the reciprocity response behavior of the Yanomamo Indians illustrates the fact of a seamless web that links those naked people whom we call savages to ourselves, the ostensibly civilized users of comparable rationalizations. Our young people of late have come to use the term "rapping" to characterize the verbal brand of this exchange. In seeing the social rituals practiced by these jungle people, I am reminded of our long since stymied talks in Paris. I am sure all of us echo Doctor Dillon's comment of the necessity of a viable alternative to unlock the stymie of our many stalled reciprocity response processes on this May Day, 1971.

At various levels of analysis, our speakers have sounded similar themes. This hints at a common dynamic that surfaces in the process of all accelerated rates of social change and episodically explodes in violence. At the level of intrapersonal dynamics, Doctor Pinderhughes suggests that the model of a shared paranoidal value system is a convenient and useful heuristic device with which to understand the complex issues that lay below these affective expressions in both individuals and group.

It has been proposed that conflict in its manifold forms has a dual objective. In the group, shared conflict multiplies the aggressive feelings of individuals and confers a certain permissiveness to the acting-out of these feelings which forcibly prosecutes its ostensible objective. Also this same force provides a necessary binding element—an interstitial social cement, as it were, which enhances in-group affiliation. This polarized state of affairs sets the stage for confrontation such as this city will demonstrate in the coming week. The magnitude and intensity of the confrontation pivots on several firmly held attitudes. There is what Doctor Pinderhughes called nonpathological paranoid behavior present in groups; the same process that Professor Hughes spoke of in its historical context and for which Doctor Dillon gave us ethnologic evidence. Then, too, there is the intrapsychic element motivating violent behavior that gives rise to the "fragging" of superior officers in Vietnam as a retaliatory reciprocity response.

Our speakers also seemed agreed that consonant with the affective response to this violent confrontation, rationalization provides the necessary catalyst in the form of moral justification. The latter is expressed in lofty, idealized terms; not unusually it asserts claims to a God-given, almost superhuman mission. This is usually said to be in behalf of such emotionally evocative issues that have cultural currency and go by the names of "democracy," "freedom," "liberty," "rights," "equality," and "brotherhood." In less secular eras than the present time, these activities were subsumed in religious terms. Thus conflicts become holy wars, jihads, crusades, vouchsafed by the Deity and alleged to be in behalf of noble ends.

They who are in opposition, by this definition, are termed "evil" and "sinful"; they are dehumanized as being immoral, bestial and thus deserving of punishment. Such stereotyping accomplishes psychological closure—the fulfillment of the rationalization because the violence that it permits is for a "good" purpose. Professor Sanford reminded us that this was the stamp of approval on all acts which intend to destroy the infidel, the unbeliever, the one who is different.

In individual psychopathology this is termed the paranoid stance. It is buttressed by the interposition of social and emotional distance from the victim. Doctor Pinderhughes suggests that this distance is an expression of a projection of the despised part of the self on denigrated others. Such displacement on a scapegoat reduces guilt as it alleviates shame and offsets the discomfort of identification.

Moreover, affectively ladened propaganda is used also to generate the requisite societal turbulence. You are familiar with the speakers' references to the trigger words which are used to create the caricatures that are typified by disparagement, distortion and derogation. These capitalize on the gross and subtle manipulative forces that employ culturally disapproved value judgments. Noblesse oblige implies that the unstated element in élitism is patronization. Perhaps this is why in these days most leadership activities are tainted by some persons with the suspicion of being establishmentarian in the worst sense. Being thus labeled, the charisma which ordinarily appends to the status of leadership is tarnished. The outgroup is thereby justified in its efforts to overthrow those in control in the name of the disenfranchised—the heretofore silent majority whom they claim to represent. Power to the people then becomes their battlecry.

To paint the picture in all its realistic complexities, it becomes necessary to add that this portrait is itself a biased view, hence an oversimplification. Indeed, there is the other side of the picture; the isolation of leadership—the very magnitude of the many problems it confronts, the volume of information overload it attempts to cope with, the necessity and fallibility of human decision-making—inevitably leads to distortion, a communications gap as we have come to call it.

Doctor Pinderhughes has recalled the fact that we see this dynamic interplay on a micro-scale in marital conflict. It is merely extrapolated in violence among large groups. These dynamics are the ingredients of the false belief system that he termed paranoidal. Doctor Pinderhughes propounds an intriguing thesis when he says it is not possible to do violence without projecting evil onto the person, group or other object of the violence. I wish there were some other term with less encrusted and pejorative connotations that one could use in a discussion of what seems to be a natural event—part and parcel of the human condition given the right circumstances and the propitious occasion.

The call for a socially valid model for human development to operate conjunctively with the several models that are propounded to account for individual psychological growth, development and maturation is long overdue. Perhaps our inquiries into the genesis of violence will adduce data which will lend themselves to testable hypotheses on the social issues that beset our times.

We have made a salutary start toward this end and it is to be hoped that in the process we will succeed in achieving what Professor Hughes called the overriding imperative of

our times: the reduction of human suffering. Education is
a fragile thread on which to hang man's hopes but it is all
we have.

Discussion

2. LOUIS JOLYON WEST, M.D.

THE PROCESS OF BEING non-élite in Pinderhughes' terms is in
some ways the same process as that of being dehumanized
in Sanford's terms. More than a decade ago, when I was
deeply involved in the early civil rights movement in Oklahoma (where, incidentally, the sit-in technique was initi-
ated) I experienced this in a very personal way.

A man awakened me with a telephone call in the middle
of the night. I recognized the voice as belonging to someone
I knew slightly; he was obviously intoxicated. He said,
"You nigger-loving bastard, we're going to come over there
and burn you out!"

I answered in a tone of voice as mild as I could muster,
"Why would you want to do something like that?" "We
figured you out," he shouted. "We figured that you're really
part black. *That* explains why you're messing around in this
business!"

By this time I was fully awake, and becoming angry. "Is
that what makes it all right for you to come over here and
destroy me?"

"Don't give me any smart talk, nigger-lover, you've only
got a few minutes to live."

I then reestablished my élite status. "Come ahead then,

you son of a bitch," I roared. "But you and your friends better be bullet-proof, because if you set foot on my property I'll blow your damn heads off!"

That was the end of the episode. Nobody came near my house that night. Downtown the next day, when the same man (sober) saw me coming down the street, he hastily turned into the nearest building.

This experience says something about the criteria for maintaining one's élite status, those days, in that neck of the woods. True, someone put a bullet through my bedroom window several weeks later, but it was a furtive gesture.

Dr. Pinderhughes and I have often discussed the dynamics of inter group prejudice and violence. I find myself in basic agreement with his formulations. His idea of the way in which projective identification leads to violence is, from my point of view, right on target. Elsewhere I have referred to this process as the formulation of the Universal Stranger. He is the one (really a group, or class) chosen by a given society at a given time as the repository for unacceptable feelings by members of that society toward their own group. The Universal Stranger (acronym, US) becomes a stereotyped object of the group's projective identifications.

"Thus it is not I who would slay my father, rape the family womenfolk, devastate the community, and destroy my own society, whose taboos and frustrating restrictions so infuriated me when I was a child. It is not I, it is the Stranger! He is of another race or nation or religion or political persuasion. The important thing is that he is different from me, and I must be sure that he *remains* a Stranger so that I cannot find out the truth: that he is as much like me as I am like myself" (1).

Dr. Pinderhughes was once the discussant for another paper of mine called *The Othello Syndrome* (2). He pointed out that it would have made just as much sense to have called the paper *The Iago Syndrome,* and I think he was right. One of the interesting points that emerged from the study of Othello was an attempt to reconstruct the extent to which, in what was probably a late 16th century English view of 15th century Venice, cultural attitudes with regard to race were not dissimilar to those in contemporary society.

As Pinderhughes noted, it's very clear in the play how Iago's paranoia becomes grossly symptomatic in Othello (who is actually a much finer, nobler person) because of the power of cultural élitism that was at work. It was a situation, to use Pinderhughes' terms, in which both the élite and the non-élite shared the delusions of the (white, Venetian) élite; both groups were unaware that their beliefs were false. So it was that Othello very easily was made to believe that his innocent wife was wicked, and even came to feel that the very fact that she could love him, black that he was, proved her to be unnatural and evil. Thus Brabantio's racist curse was fulfilled, and violence followed.

In considering the prospect of alternatives to violence, Dr. Pinderhughes calls our attention to something very important. He points out the constantly changing complexion of power, and the corresponding flux of necessity for projection, in developmental terms. The phenomenon of infantile omnipotence suggests that the human developmental dichotomy between the brain's capacity to comprehend and the body's inability to survive (which is also comprehended) teaches the child at an early age that he is *not* omnipotent, that he is, in fact, virtually helpless. As Pinderhughes might say, the child discovers that he is non-élite, while adults are élite.

It becomes apparent that if alternatives to violence are to be developed, we must proceed by looking at individuals from the viewpoint of growth and development. When we do so, attention should be paid to the developmental vicissitudes of infantile omnipotence as it becomes submerged, transformed, and manifested again in adulthood in various disguises. The dynamics of this process have been elegantly analyzed by Pumpian-Mindlin (3).

Furthermore, while we are considering the natural development of the individual in relationship to his propensities for violence (and, hopefully, his potential resources in finding alternatives to violence), we must not fail to reflect on the temporal development of groups. A growing concern with group dynamics reveals that, like any other organism, each group (or culture, or society, or family, or mob, or infantry squad) has a natural history of its own, which is unique but similar—perhaps sequentially—to all others. Disparate as various societies may be, from the developmental point of view there may be an inevitable order imposed on their growth. If so, this order probably derives from the biosocial characteristics of the individuals comprising the group. If this be true it could follow (as I have suggested elsewhere) that the capacities of groups both for self-righteous slaughter of others, and for ethical concern and devotion to others, may finally be comprehended in scientific terms.

"It has finally come to pass, after perhaps 20 million years of human evolution, that in our lifetime there is finally defined, by every government of men in the world, the principle that human slavery is *wrong*. . . . Here is an ethic. Its derivation will, I believe, be demonstrable through basic biosocial research on human development. From such studies a proposition like the following might follow. The child passes through the stage of master in his infantile omnipotence and then through the stage of slave when his rapidly maturing brain chafes at his childish body's weak and helpless dependence upon adults who—to whatever extent they choose—are his rulers. Adolescent rebellion is man's eternal struggle for freedom. Every normal person experiences these phases, thus knowing in his heart the anguish of slavery, the sickness of desiring it for others or oneself, and the health of casting it off. If human misery is termed 'bad,' and health "good," then slavery is unethical and everyone knows it. . . . Ultimately we may find that sociogeny recapitulates ontogeny, which recapitulates phylogeny" (4).

Returning to Pinderhughes' terminology we should remember that, while much violence is generated in struggles between élite and non-élite groups within any organization, it often transpires in human affairs that each of two opposing organizations considers itself to be élite. In fact, regardless of the superficial positions of each with regard to any particular criterion—wealth, for instance, the self-view of the antagonist is that he and his kind are superior in the most important ways to the enemy. It even appears that élitism of one type (e.g. Nationalism) may influence people to accept more compliantly a non-élite status closer to home (e.g. economic deprivation).

Professor Dillon has reminded us that a great deal of current thinking about enmity has been postulated in terms of instinctual territoriality and the aggression that accompanies it. I agree with him, and with others who have been inspecting and then rejecting this attractive but superficial hypothesis. It seems most likely that man is not a basically territorial animal. Neither, for that matter, are the elephant, the whale, nor the gorilla, to name three of my favorite mammalian cousins who are much more like man than are the mocking bird, the antelope, or the wasp.

The proposition of inevitable violence through territoriality, suggested by Lorenz and popularized by Ardrey, also states that psychiatrists and psychologists are far off the mark when they maintain that all of man's hostile interactions with his own kind are ramifications of "love." Here Ardrey (obviously without having investigated the psychoanalytic literature) takes Freud's "libido" theory at semantic face value. Ardrey contends that we in psychiatry and psychology have abandoned the useful concept of instinct; apparently he fails to understand that the concept of *conflict* between instinctive drives and learned constraints is basic to the structure of modern psychodynamics.

Ardrey goes on to suggest that territoriality leads men to war, thus proving itself to be a more potent force than "the will to survive, the sexual impulse, the tie . . . between mother and infant." He suggests that, ". . . We may test the supposition with a single question: How many men have you known of, in your lifetime, who died for their country? And how many for a woman?" (5). Clearly, according to Ardrey, it is the territorial imperative that leads to violence and aggression.

A gifted and persuasive writer but not a behavioral scientist, Ardrey thus shows the dangers inherent in extrapolating not only from animals to humans, but from animal organizations to human armies. Having served in uniform in varying capacities for nearly a dozen years, it is my view that, while it may be true that "men have died from time to time, and worms have eaten them, but not for love," very few people die for their territory, either. Students of military psychology have studied the motivation of soldiers going back as far as the Trojan War (which was probably fought neither for Helen nor for Troy). It is clear that people can be induced to behave contrary to their most powerful instincts, including those of hunger, thirst, sex, the avoidance of pain, the pursuit of pleasure, and even self-preservation (not to mention territoriality, since most men die in war far from home), only if there is an overriding motive.

Such motivation usually has to do with role, status, social pressure, and the dynamics of the group—usually a small group of individuals who have been in close contact for some time. With and for these men, a man will do what he finds at the moment of danger that it is necessary to do, that they expect him to do, that he'd be ashamed not to do. Thus Dillon's approach, in contrast to theorizing about man from animal behavior, seems to me intensely important, heuristic, and philosophically valid. *La vraie science et la vraie étude de l'homme, c'est l'homme.*

Dillon suggests that we inspect situations in which Nature has already conducted the experiments; in which human beings under certain culturally consistent or circumscribed conditions have demonstrated techniques for the resolution of conflict which have worked, and which can be shown to succeed, to avoid violence in human transactions. The example Dillon gives us is most instructive. Finding such experiments of Nature, however, is far from easy.

In a long study of problems of violence, I have often been disappointed in my investigation of cultures or societies which have been represented as free from aggression or violence. Once I tried to study the meager record of life in Polynesia before the arrival of white men, a period and place often described as a human paradise. I discovered, however, that this legendary paradise was not quite so halcyon as the most romantic accounts would have us believe. The famous landing and warm welcome of Captain James Cook to Tahiti in 1769 is a case in point. Cook, with his magical-seeming ship, muskets, and cannon, was welcomed enthusiastically, not in a spirit of brotherly love by unspoiled peaceful flower people, but rather as a potential ally of a group of Tahitians who were at war with other Tahitians at the opposite end of their heavenly island at the time. The similarity of this experience to Gulliver's relation to the Lilliputians in their war against their blood-brothers gives added respect for the ironical insights of Jonathan Swift into human nature, nearly half a century before Captain Cook set sail in the *Endeavour*.

Recently, however, I have had the good fortune to study a culture that is singularly free of aggression and violence. The Tarahumara Indians inhabit a particularly bleak part of Mexico, the Sierra Madre Occidental. It has been possible to gather some fascinating data about their unusually peaceful, semi-agrarian, semi-nomadic way of life. What I have learned may be instructive in terms of our concern today with alternatives to violence.

There are about 50,000 Tarahumara living on the high plateaus and in the barrancas of the Sierra Madre. They may be the largest group of North American Indians that remains relatively unchanged by the pressures of western "progress." They speak a Uto-Aztec tongue, but had no written language until Jesuit missionaries recently created one phonetically. In the last 25 years, during which fairly reliable records have been kept by these missionaries, among these 50,000 Indians, crime, delinquency, and significant interpersonal violence (either among themselves or toward outsiders) has been virtually unknown. Over the same quarter-century we know of not a single suicide, and only one or two homicides. The latter apparently were inadvertent consequences of drunken unarmed fights during *tesguinada*. In the Tarahumara country there are no soldiers, no police, and no jails.

These Indians are warm and friendly, possess a marvelous sense of humor, but are also dignified and treat each other with great respect. They are impressive athletes, probably the world's greatest long-distance runners. I have seen two ten-year-old Tarahumara boys run a 26-mile race (by coincidence, the Olympic marathon distance) each kicking a wooden ball the entire distance. Small teams of male adults commonly race for distances of 80 to 160 miles, each team kicking its ball along mountain trails at altitudes of 7,000 feet.

I agree with Dr. Dillon's proposition that an exchange of gifts of genuine value between people constitutes one mechanism through which an alternative to violence may become a way of life. In another form this phenomenon is perhaps to some degree demonstrable among the Tarahumara, even though there is no ceremonial gift-giving. What then do they give each other?

For one thing, the Tarahumara take possessions seriously, yet don't value them excessively. Nothing is owned in common, no one acquires anything by marriage, each spouse retains his own property. It passes to another individual only by inheritance, sale, wager, or gift. The Tarahumara are great bettors, and love to wager on the outcome of sporting contests, especially the kick-ball races. They can ill afford to lose, but accept their losses without rancor.

Another important thing Tarahumara give each other is the *tesguinada*. Festive occasions bringing great pleasure and satisfaction, these gatherings are periodically sponsored by individuals for their neighbors. There is dancing, music, sport, talk, and much drinking of the local corn beer, *tesguino*. These parties may last for several days. They provide rituals within the tribal folkways which help to perpetuate the culture, to preserve and pass along its important legends and mores, and also to create interludes of group enjoyment and fun among people whose life is otherwise hard.

The most important thing each person can give, which lies behind the Tarahumara love for the *tesguinada* and the foot race, is himself. For the Tarahumara are scattered across a vast, bleak, infertile and remote country. The low yield of the soil and the sparseness of the foliage compel them to live in comparative isolation. Their life is a continual struggle against nature, and their only help comes from each other.

The supreme value of persons in the fight to survive is something of which each Tarahumara is well aware. Furthermore, the importance of the child in the survival of the family is crucial. The rate of infant mortality is high, and each child is cherished and valued. The Tarahumara don't beat their children; they avoid inflicting pain, and never deliberately deprive a child of anything necessary to his security or satisfaction. Yet their children are remarkably well-behaved.

How do these children learn discipline and self-control? Through laughter. If a child does something he shouldn't do, the adults will look at him in astonishment and burst into laughter. The child hangs his head in shame; he is most unlikely to repeat his error or transgression. Here, then, is a culture in which guilt is not employed as the primary instrument for regulation of the individual by the group. Shame seems to be the principal mechanism of control.

In this context I would like to add another interesting psychiatric observation. In a culture where drinking to intoxication is basic to the primary (and frequent) social ceremony, one might expect alcoholism to be a problem (as it is among so many North American Indians). In point of fact, however, alcoholism is virtually unknown among the mountain Tarahumara (6).

In a recent paper, *The Place of Value in a World of Facts,* read at the 14th Nobel Symposium in Stockholm, Arthur Koestler seriously questioned whether mankind is endangered as much by innate savagery as by the obsolescence of his biosocial adaptive characteristics, especially the capacity for sentiment, and the excessive identification with groups: the need to belong and to conform. The challenging idea here is that the motivating force behind even such events as the My Lai massacre is not territoriality, not instinctual violence, but love. Koestler in his own way makes the point that Professor Sanford has made so well in this symposium. It is that man's proclivity to go out and slaughter large numbers of other men doesn't seem to be based on primitive savagery, but rather seems to stem from passive, rather dependant, group-oriented, and affectional concern for other human beings close to him. It depends as well on human susceptibility to shibboleths held in common, on the differential development in many of the neocortex in relationship to the paleocortex (and the consequent peculiar split between rational thought and emotional belief), on the guilt-derived concept of sacrifice, and on the singular lack of instinctive *prevention* of killing one's own kind.

These peculiarly human tendencies are compounded, through language, by cultures which are thus able to keep alive within themselves shibboleths, institutions and commitments. Even when these are seldom acted out, they nevertheless remain (in theory at least) as a part of the accepted body of beliefs of that culture. A reference has been made by Professor Sanford to the death penalty. In America today, the anachronism of capital punishment provides a vivid example of this phenomenon. We no longer want to exercise the death penalty in our culture; it is obviously futile and barbaric. But we don't want to strike it from the books, either. We cling to it as a primitive symbol of our willingness to carry out, as a group, an act considered immoral and illegal for any individual: the deliberate putting to death of a helpless captive.

Similarly, the desire to band together to attack other groups remains institutionalized. When we look for the circumstances under which this sanction is likely to be carried out, we make an interesting discovery. The people most likely to organize in this way are not the impatient hotheads, the fiery young rebels. The rebellious youth are not the ones who calculate coldly and objectively the number of mega-deaths that can be tolerated by one side in order to defeat the other. The men in the political and military power élite who make such plans and decisions are usually the most respectable, well-established, and successful members of any society. The rebels, while they are widely feared and cele-brated as prone to violence, and while stern measures are taken to secure society against them, are boy scouts by com-parison.

Violence in the world today does not begin or end on the campus. And, despite the depredations of a few zealots, the rebels—of whatever persuasion—are not a major source of violence. Nor can we use fluctuating figures relating to indi-vidual crimes of violence to distract ourselves from the truly monumental issues of inter-group violence in the world.

Punjabi against Bengali in East Pakistan; Catholic against Protestant in Ulster; Hausa against Ibo in Nigeria; Malay against Chinese in Indonesia; North against South in Korea and Vietnam; Greek against Turk in Cyprus; Hindu against Moslem in Kashmir; Arab against Jew in the Levant; African against "coloured" in Zanzibar; white against black in America; nation against nation any time, any place: when the final log book of destruction of masses of people by other masses of people is compiled, it will surely appear that the fateful violence was engendered far more often by respectable leaders than by rebellious youths at college. It will develop that intolerably oppressive circumstances lead-ing to crimes of desperation, or outbursts of revolutionary fire, were perpetrated and maintained by the most dignified and accepted personages and institutions of the time. It will become clear, at last, that it is conformity, not rebelliousness, that can be indicted in the psychodynamic infrastructure of man's major violent propensities toward man.

It is the conformist, not the rebel, into whose hands the power of any well-established society is likely to be passed. And it is the conformist who is most likely to preserve precisely those characteristics of the society that will perpetuate prejudice and privilege within it, and a warlike disposition toward others. Ironically, it is all too soon that within any society a given mode of rebellion becomes institutionalized, demanding conformity of its adherents, and orienting itself toward outsiders in the same arrogance of righteousness that distinguished its progenitor. Then, once again, conformist versus conformist, implacable inter-group violence is forthcoming.

Nevertheless, the rebellious spirit is the moving force of whatever progress it is possible for human organizations to accomplish. We need our rebels in this world, now more than ever before. The gravest danger today in America—and everywhere—is that rebellious youth will be crushed by the panic reaction of masses of conformists, aroused to terrible repressiveness in response to a few outrageous actions spewed forth by the lunatic fringe of rebellion. Caught in the crossfire, more and more of those would-be rebels who are repelled by violence will surely turn to the more passive "hippie" counter-culture to escape.

This flight from violence is carrying thousands of our youth into experimentation with alternative life-styles as alternatives to violence. Even the use of drugs in many of the contemporary communes (which are perhaps better termed utopian societies) is often found to serve, at least in part, the need for conflict resolution to preserve the group (7).

To my mind it becomes increasingly clear that mankind's hope of survival lies in development of greater understanding of biosocial universals, and the application of this knowledge to child rearing practices, public education, and group dynamics. To such an understanding we in psychiatry clearly can contribute.

REFERENCES

1. WEST, L. J., "Psychobiology of Racial Violence," *Archives Gen. Psych.* Volume 16, 645-651, June 1967.
2. WEST, L. J., "The Othello Syndrome," *Contemporary Psychoanalysis,* 4:2, 103-110, 1968.
3. PUMPIAN-MINDLIN, E., "Vicissitudes of Infantile Omnipotence," in *Psychoanalytic Study of the Child,* Int. Univ. Press, Volume XXIV, 1969.
4. WEST, L. J., "Ethical Psychiatry and Biosocial Humanism," *Amer. J. Psychiat.* 126:2, August 1969.
5. ARDREY, R., *The Territorial Imperative.* New York: Atheneum, 1966, p. 7.
6. WEST, L. J., PAREDES, A., and SNOW, C. C., "Sanity in the Sierra Madre: The Tarahumara Indians," presented at 122nd Annual Meeting, American Psychiatric Association, Miami Beach, Florida, May 1969.
7. WEST, L. J., "Flight from Violence II: The Communes," presented at 124th Annual Meeting, American Psychiatric Association, Washington, D.C., May 1971.